SPECIAL F S0-BLN-847
SPORTING
GUNS

SPECIAL FORCES
SPORTING
GUNS

WEAPONS, SKILLS, AND TECHNIQUES
FOR COMPETITIVE SHOOTING SPORTS

MARTIN J. DOUGHERTY

METRO BOOKS
New York

METRO BOOKS
New York

An Imprint of Sterling Publishing
387 Park Avenue South
New York, NY 10016

METRO BOOKS and the distinctive Metro Books logo are trademarks
of Sterling Publishing Co., Inc.

Editorial and design by
Amber Books Ltd
74–77 White Lion Street
London N1 9PF
www.amberbooks.co.uk

Project Editor: Michael Spilling
Designer: MRM Graphics
Picture Research: Terry Forshaw
Illustrations: Tony Randell

Additional text by Chris McNab.

ISBN: 978-1-4351-5340-0

For information about custom editions, special sales, and premium and corporate purchases,
please contact Sterling Special Sales at 800-805-5489 or specialsales@sterlingpublishing.com.

Manufactured in Malaysia

2 4 6 8 10 9 7 5 3 1

www.sterlingpublishing.com

DISCLAIMER

This book is for information purposes only. Readers should be aware of the legal position
in their country of residence before practicing any of the techniques described in this
book. Neither the author or the publisher can accept responsibility for any loss, injury, or
damage caused as a result of the use of the techniques described in this book, nor for any
prosecutions or proceedings brought or instigated against any person or body that may
result from using these techniques.

CONTENTS

The term 'sporting guns' is generally used to refer to all firearms that are not intended for use as weapons against people. That does not mean that they cannot be pressed into service for home or personal defence, or accidentally harm someone, but their primary purpose is not for combat. Similarly, 'gun sports' include pretty much all firearms activity that is not primarily intended for hurting people or training to do so.

Beyond that, the field is very varied and gun sports differ sufficiently from one another that an entirely different set of skills may be needed. Gun sports range from target shooting for amusement or competitive purposes to hunting and vermin control. Some of these activities are not, strictly speaking, sports – hunting can put food on the table, and keeping down vermin protects crops – but they do fall within the same general set of activities and use the same tools.

Choosing the Right Gun

The equipment required, as well as the skillset in use, varies from one field to another. Any gun can be used for a bit of target shooting, but

....

There is more to hunting than marksmanship. Understanding the quarry and its environment enables the hunter to maximize his advantages with the right camouflage and decoys.

1

Gun sports range from casual plinking at targets to Olympic-standard shooting matches, and from fun activities like Cowboy Action Shooting to realistic combat simulation events.

Gun Sports and Sporting Guns

Types of Sporting Gun

From top: bolt-action rifle, semi-automatic shotgun, double-barrelled shotgun. Each offers the user clear advantages in the right role.

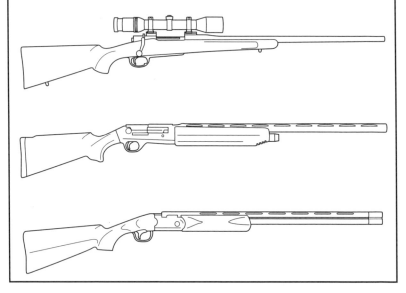

for serious competition a specialist firearm is needed. Target pistols and rifles are extremely precise instruments that might not take kindly to being dragged through the wilderness in search of game, even if they are effective in that role. A gun designed for putting down large targets such as turkey or deer might not be well suited to hunting small game, and might constitute

overkill for vermin control. There are also legal considerations. Permit requirements and local gun laws can force the choice of weapon. In some areas, for example, it is legal to hunt with a shotgun but not a rifle. If it is necessary to bring down quite robust targets, such as turkey, from a fair distance, then a shotgun might not be ideal. The way around this is to use specialist ammunition that extends accurate range and knockdown power while remaining within the bounds of the law.

The majority of sporting guns are not ideally suited to home defence or personal protection applications. Any gun is better than no gun of course, but in most cases it is better to have a gun for sport and a gun for defence rather than compromising effectiveness in one area in case your chosen weapon has to be pressed into service for the other.

As a general rule, shotguns are used for hunting birds and small, fast-moving animals, and for sports that parallel these activities such as clay pigeon shooting. Shotguns can be used with specialist ammunition for hunting larger game in areas where rifles are not permitted, or to avoid having to carry more than one gun on a shoot. Rifles are generally used for longer-range shooting, with heavier calibres used for deer and similar large game, and smaller calibres being more suitable for smaller game. Some very large calibre rifles are available for hunting dangerous game, but this is a specialist activity.

Rifles are also popular for target shooting, as are pistols. Indeed, target shooting is the main sporting activity undertaken with handguns, although some hunters prefer to use them either for their ease of carry compared to a rifle or to increase the challenge. Within these general categories there is an almost infinite variety of equipment that can be tailored to both the application you have in mind and your preferences as the user.

Thus a sporting gun should be chosen based on what you intend to do with it, but it is always worth remembering that gun sports, with a few exceptions, are not just about shooting. The gun you choose is the gun you will have to carry… and buy ammunition for… and clean… and obtain the right permits for… and a host of other tasks that are not really anything to do with actually firing it.

User Friendly

When you choose a piece of equipment you should be mindful of who it's for. The absolute best gun for, say, shooting waterfowl, may not be the best gun to carry and use on a waterfowling shoot. Your kit must be suited to the user, and not to some abstract standard of what is 'better'.

Some shooters, like people in every other field, will define themselves by the equipment they have. Brands are important, price tags sometimes even more so. Some shooters will cite chapter and verse from reviews or shooting books as proof that they are somehow superior because they own the piece of equipment being praised or know the technique described. This is a rather false standard, however. The real test is how well you can perform with the

On a Shoot

Many hunters choose to work with an experienced guide, who can show them where to find the game they seek and offer advice as needed. Guides may be experts-for-hire or an experienced hunter might take on the role for his friends.

equipment you have, and whether you find the shooting experience enjoyable, fulfilling or successful in other ways. It is results, not possessions, that count.

In order to obtain good results it is necessary to work towards them. That means mastering your gun and instinctively knowing how it performs, but also knowing what you need to do in order to make an effective shot. You can hone your precision shooting to a fine pitch on the firing range, but if all the ducks fly away when you come crashing through the undergrowth then your marksmanship is worthless. A little time spent on fieldcraft rather than attaining an incredible standard of marksmanship under perfect conditions will pay dividends.

Thus the sporting shooter that understands his equipment and the requirements of his sport – and has the right skills – will vastly outperform someone who lacks specialist knowledge even if his opponent is a better marksman under perfect conditions. However, the basic principles of weapon handling and marksmanship are common to all gun sports – putting the shot where you want it is what it's all about.

Safety

The first duty of any gun book is to reiterate the principles of firearms safety. Like the safety briefing aboard an aircraft, these can often

Secure Your Guns!

It may seem obvious that loaded guns should not be left lying about, yet it does happen. A weapon that is not in use should be securely stored, not only to prevent accidents but also to make it difficult to steal. A gun rack in a locked room, or a gun safe, is sufficient to control access to a weapon – which should of course be stored unloaded. Ammunition can usually be stored with the weapon, although in some localities there are legal requirements to store ammunition separately.

Controlling access to your guns is especially important where there are children in the home. Even if you have none of your own, you cannot guarantee that at some point you will not have visitors. It is possible to forget about a hazard that does not normally exist, but controlling access ensures that mistakes cannot be made.

Gun Storage

A gun safe controls access to weapons and ammunition, and also provides a tidy place to put all your associated gear like goggles and ear defenders. If it's all in one place you will be less likely to forget something when you go out shooting.

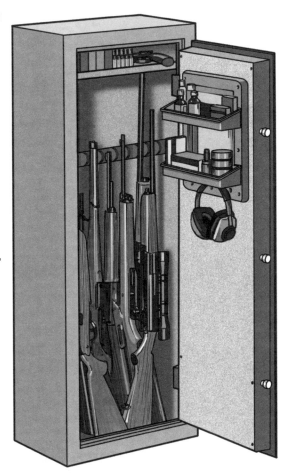

be treated casually. Thousands of people die every year in shooting accidents, yet almost every incident could be prevented with basic safety measures. These are:

- Treat every gun as if it was loaded. On picking up any weapon, make sure that it is empty by breaking open the action or opening the bolt.
- Never point the muzzle at anything you wouldn't be prepared to shoot.
- Keep the safety on at all times, and your finger off the trigger, until you are ready to shoot.
- Understand how your gun works. Spend time with the user guide and also, vitally, be clear about what ammunition type your gun will take. Keep the gun clean and well maintained.
- If you pull the trigger and the gun doesn't go off, point it at a safe place and do nothing for

up to 30 seconds. Then unload the gun.
- Check the barrel of the gun for obstructions before you shoot, and do the same if the barrel of the gun has come into contact with mud or earth.
- Don't load the weapon until you are ready to shoot. Keep the gun safely stored so that unauthorized people cannot get access it. This is particularly important if there are children in the house.
- Be aware of what is beyond your target. Remember that you can miss and that some bullets can pass through prey and continue their flight for a long distance. Make sure your shot has a solid stop in the background.
- When hunting in a pair or group, be continually aware of where everyone else is, and set

Choosing a Gun

Although the final decision about what model to buy can be complex, the process is simplified by considering what you want the gun to do, which in turn suggests calibre or gauge. Considerations of your own physical characteristics and the available budget will narrow your choices to a few weapons. Of course, this process applies mainly to practical shooters. Those who consider a gun to be a fashion accessory or conversation piece will usually just pay over the odds for a good name and beautiful decoration, basing the choice on what they think will impress their peers.

Safe Handling

**Safe weapon carry and handling comes down to
making sure that the weapon cannot fire and,
even if it somehow does, that it is pointed in
a direction where it will not injure anyone.**

Cylinder open

Breech open,
muzzle pointed
towards ground

Finger outside
trigger guard

generous margins of error for
how much swing you will allow
yourself before abandoning the
shot because other people
are too close.

- Never use anything that
  impairs your mental focus
  while shooting, particularly
  alcohol or drugs (prescription
  or otherwise).

Responsibility and the Law

Following these rules strictly will ensure your shooting experience is safe and enjoyable. Shooters must be models of responsibility if the sport is to survive. This is particularly important in hunting. Hunters should only shoot another living species if a) it is lawful (read up on national, state and local legislation); b) there is a legitimate purpose, such as pest control, authorized culls or for food; and c) if they have the skill to do so. If you hunt, try to eat or use everything you kill. Hunters should find out as much about nature as they can, because, despite the frequent public perception, most good shooters are passionately interested in conservation.

Responsible shooting also means owning and using firearms within the limits of the law. Check out all district, state and national laws before purchasing a firearm, and ensure that all the correct paperwork is filed promptly with the authorities. Remember that gun laws vary dramatically between states and countries, particularly with regard to transportation and storage of firearms, and the places guns can be used, so find out about legal variations prior to making a journey with your gun.

Be particularly careful if taking your gun abroad on a sporting trip – it may be best to hire guns abroad to avoid the complex mass of paperwork it requires to transport firearms. Be aware that falling foul of a gun law can result in serious penalties, including imprisonment, so take legal issues very seriously.

Clothing and Accessories

It is extremely important to be suitably dressed whenever you head out into the countryside or undertake

Guns and Alcohol

Many shooters believe that there is no safe level of alcohol in the bloodstream when handling a firearm. Alcohol impairs both coordination and judgement, making the shooter at the same time more likely to do something irresponsible and also less competent. In some areas, drinking is considered part of the social aspect of shooting but it is usually wise to steer clear of anyone who thinks that booze and guns are a good mix.

Ghillie Suit

A Ghillie suit is designed to break up the human outline and turn the wearer into a shapeless vegetation-like mass.

Specialist Clothing

Specialist clothing is not 100 per cent necessary of course, but it has been developed to meet the needs of shooters in terms of ease of movement, layout of pockets and so forth.

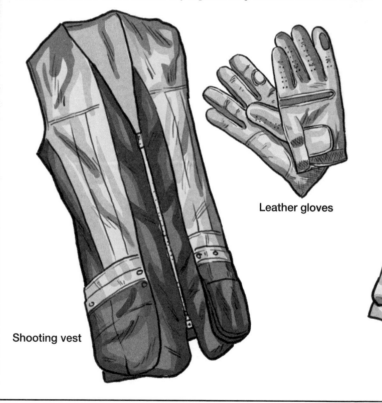

Leather gloves

Shooting vest

any outdoor pursuit. Standing around on a clay pigeon range on a wet January day is an exercise in misery without warm, dry and windproof clothing. Buying the right clothing is a matter of safety as well as comfort, and will affect your performance in many ways. There is also usually a

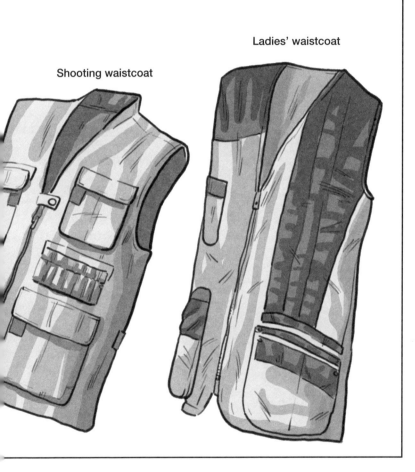

Ladies' waistcoat

Shooting waistcoat

desire to 'look the part' that goes beyond not advertising your presence to every duck within a day's flight in every direction. Shooting often has a social context, and if you feel that you stand out as an outsider or a 'newbie' then you will be uncomfortable even if nobody thinks any less of you for

Headgear

Headgear can be very important in cold or sunny conditions, and can be useful in breaking up the distinctive outline of the human head or at least camouflaging it a bit.

Shooting Goggles

Shooting goggles often come with swappable clear and tinted lenses. They offer protection not only from weapon malfunctions or ejected shells, but also from wind-blown dust, grit and vegetation.

your choice of apparel. If you are uncomfortable then you will be tense, and that will affect your shooting. So, in the end, looking the part can actually improve your performance on a shoot, or at least prevent it being needlessly degraded.

Some items are sold specifically as 'shooting apparel' but the most important aspects of your kit are that it should be warm, dry and comfortable to wear. Clothes that restrict your movement are not a good choice, and you do not want to be fumbling about

in awkwardly sited pockets while trying to reload. Thus it is well worth trying on any item you are considering buying, not merely from the point of view of fit but also utility.

There are some parts of the world where you might be expected to show up at a shoot in a nice tweed suit, and tweed is still favoured by some shooters for its warmth and durability. However, as a rule, practical outdoor clothing in a sensible muted colour (that basically means green and/or brown) will suffice. Camouflage is useful for stalking game, but for, say, a pheasant shoot it is only necessary not to stand out against the natural landscape. It is worth asking about clothing requirements for a type of shoot you are not familiar with, or for a group you have not shot with before. Some shooters are very relaxed about apparel; others have more rules than a military academy.

Footwear is important on any shoot in the countryside. Boots or stout walking shoes are essential in most areas, and the traditional green wellingtons with industrial-grade socks are advisable in cold and wet moorland or forest environments. Similarly, gloves can be essential to keep your hands functional on a cold day, and also provide protection from nature's endless assault with splinters, thorns and deceptively razor-edged rocks. A hat may be a good idea to keep the sun out of your eyes and off your head, and for warmth. A baseball cap is entirely acceptable under most circumstances, although again there are those who expect more traditional headgear.

Accessories

A vast array of accessories are available, ranging from extremely useful to the somewhat silly. For certain types of shooting some accessories can improve the chances of success, such as decoys and duck calls, and the experienced shooter knows how to make good use of them. Most other accessories are a matter of preference or comfort, and some are basically on the market to make money from people who want to look like experienced shooters. Having a basketful of gadgets is not a substitute for knowing what you are doing, however, and there are few accessories that you really need.

Apart from eye and ear protection, you also need some way to carry ammunition that is convenient and minimizes fumbling about with cold hands. A cartridge belt or bag makes it easy to get at ammunition when you want it, and saves emptying out your pockets after a shoot. Apart from this, accessories are very much a matter of personal preference. Some modify your weapon or fit it more perfectly to your use, such as recoil pads. Experience will indicate which you want – if any – and how to make best use of them.

It is worth noting the tendency of some accessory manufacturers to stick the word 'tactical' on virtually everything. 'Tactical' accessories are generally aimed at the self-defence shooting end of the market and competitions that emulate it, such as practical pistol events, but some shooters feel the need to possess all manner of tactical items. In truth it does not matter all that much if your underpants are tactical or not.

Similarly, if you decide that you

U.S. Army Tip – Winter Clothing

C – keep clothing clean. Clothes matted with dirt and grease lose much of their insulation value. Heat can escape more easily from the body through the clothing's crushed or filled-up air pockets.

O – avoid overheating. Adjust your clothing so that you do not sweat. Do this by partially opening your parka or jacket, by removing an inner layer of clothing, by removing heavy outer mittens or by throwing back your parka hood or changing to lighter headgear. The head and hands act as efficient heat dissipaters when overheated.

L – wear your clothing loose and in layers. Several layers of lightweight clothing are better than one equally thick layer of clothing, because the layers have dead-air space between them. The dead-air space provides extra insulation. Also, layers of clothing allow you to take off or add layers to prevent excessive sweating or to increase warmth.

D – keep clothing dry. Wear water repellent outer clothing if available. Before entering a heated shelter, brush off the snow and frost. On the march, hang your damp mittens and socks on your rucksack. You can also place damp socks or mittens, unfolded, near your body so that your body heat can dry them. In a campsite, hang damp clothing inside the shelter near the top, using drying lines or improvised racks. You may even be able to dry an item by holding it before an open fire.

want items like ground sheets, umbrellas and similar peripherals, then you may be able to get what you need at a much lower price in a sporting goods or outdoor store than from a dedicated shooting accessories supplier. Some of the latter seem to work on the assumption that people who will pay thousands for a good gun are equally

Accessories

Accessories are more than fashion statements. They allow a weapon to be tailored to the user's exact specification, ammunition to be conveniently carried, and a host of other minor conveniences that are only noticed when they are not there.

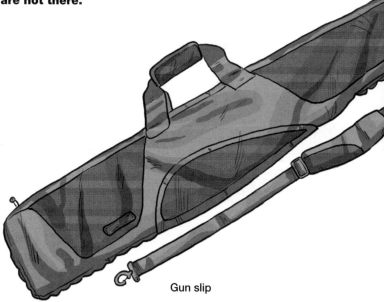

Gun slip

willing to spend a lot on an umbrella, and there is a certain amount of brand recognition, as with any other market sector. The truth is that if your kit is functional and the design is not too embarrassing, then it is not all

that relevant where you bought it.

As with all your shooting equipment, what matters is that your gear should be robust, reliable, comfortable to wear or easy to use, and well suited to its purpose. There

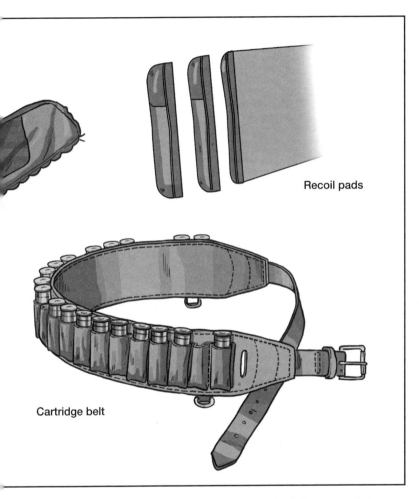

Recoil pads

Cartridge belt

is a big difference between getting an accessory because you think it will improve your shooting or your enjoyment of it – or reduce the effects of inclement weather – and buying an expensive piece of kit because you think you should have one. Get some experience or at least good advice before spending money on an item you may not really need, or which you may have to replace with a more practical alternative soon afterwards.

At the risk of stating the obvious, it is important to have the right gun for what you intend to do. It is possible to muddle through with a barely adequate firearm or one that is optimized for a different application, but the likely result is frustration and a poor performance. In some cases it is possible to fall foul of the law by using a weapon for the wrong purpose and, in a social context, some shooters can be disparaging of 'newbies' who bring the wrong gun to a shoot. It is also necessary to understand how your weapon works and why it might malfunction.

Firearms of all types have a number of components in common. They need a firing chamber and a mechanism to fire the ammunition, a barrel to guide the projectile and some means to hold the weapon. Rifles and shotguns have a shoulder stock; handguns have only a grip. One key factor in precise shooting is stability of the weapon. A rifle or shotgun pulled in snugly to the shoulder is inevitably more stable than a handgun, although a good stance goes a long way towards improving stability.

• •

A shooter's faith in his gun is important to making a clean shot; mistrust leads to mistakes. The answer is to look after your gun and to work in partnership with it.

2

An excellent gun will not make a poor shot any better, but a poor gun will cause anyone to underperform. Weapon selection and maintenance are every bit as important as marksmanship.

Know Your Gun

Varieties of Sporting Guns

Military-style weapons can be used for sport and hunting of course, but most sporting guns follow a traditional layout.

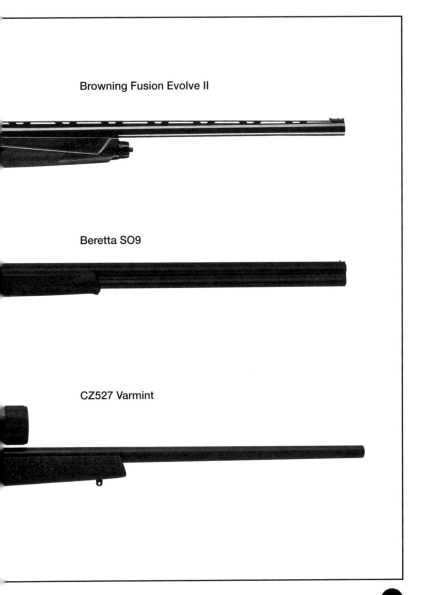

Browning Fusion Evolve II

Beretta SO9

CZ527 Varmint

Types of Ammo

Ammunition consists of four main components: Projectile(s), propellant, case and primer. Although rifle and shotgun ammunition look quite different, both are basically the same in principle.

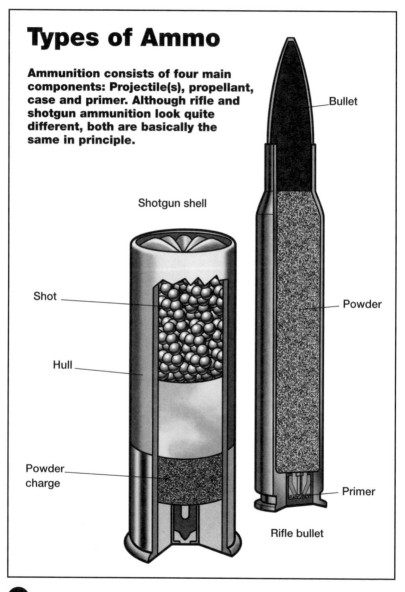

Shotgun shell

Bullet

Shot

Powder

Hull

Powder charge

Primer

Rifle bullet

The inside of a weapon's barrel is known as the bore. The end through which the projectile leaves the weapon is termed the muzzle, while the end of the barrel that contains the firing chamber is called the breech. Length of barrel contributes directly to accuracy; a longer barrel improves the weapon's precision. Shotguns barrels are normally smooth; those of pistols and rifles have curved grooves (known as rifling) cut into them to impart spin to the projectile as it moves down the barrel.

Sights are essential to accurate shooting at any great distance, but for applications such as clay pigeon shooting or fowling, a simple bead foresight is entirely sufficient. Most guns come with a basic set of 'iron sights', which typically consist of a blade foresight and a notch rear sight, which can be adjusted for shooting at greater distances. Many rifles are manufactured with the ability to take a telescopic sight, while some come with one as standard.

Rimfire and Centrefire

A centrefire cartridge has its primer in the centre of the base, where it is struck by the firing pin. Rimfire rounds have their primer around the base instead. This configuration is generally used in small-calibre weapons.

Weapons Types

Some kinds of action are better suited to some weapons than others. Revolver-carbines have been constructed, for example, but the configuration never caught on.

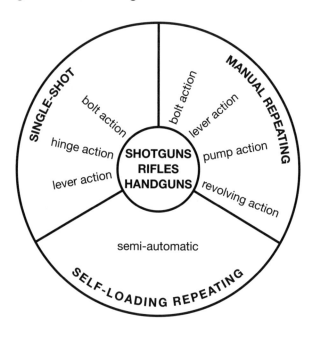

Characteristics

All modern firearms work on the same general principles. Ammunition takes the form of a unitary (one-piece) cartridge in the case of pistols and rifles. The projectile (bullet) is held at the front of the cartridge, whose case is filled with propellant. The case is normally of metal, and can sometimes be reused by reloading it with propellant and fitting a new bullet. The propellant is initiated by a smaller explosion created when the primer is struck by the weapon's hammer or firing pin. The primer can be embedded in the base of the cartridge case, an arrangement referred to as 'centre-fire', or can be around the rim. This is predictably called 'rimfire'. The primer is less stable than the bulk of the propellant, and is designed to detonate if struck, whereas the main propellant will not. It may 'cook off' if it gets hot enough, but this is extremely unlikely in a sporting gun, so the only way to make a weapon discharge is to strike the primer.

In the case of shotguns, the ammunition is known as a shell and the cartridge case is replaced with a soft (usually plastic) hull that contains propellant and has a primer at the base. Shotguns typically fire a pattern of spherical shot of varying weight depending on the purpose they are intended for, but can use a range of specialist ammunition. Shot is held in the shell by a wad, typically of paper, plastic or fibre, which keeps the shot and propellant from becoming intermixed and helps make a good gas seal during firing. Ammunition is held in the firing chamber and struck to initiate it, at which point the propellant in the main charge deflagrates (burns extremely rapidly) and creates a large volume of hot gas. Since the chamber is sealed, this creates very high gas pressure that pushes the only part that can move – the projectile – down the barrel.

Bullet Dynamics

The more propellant is in the cartridge, the greater the volume of hot gas produced and thus the greater the chamber pressure. Excessive chamber pressures can cause damage to a gun or even catastrophic failure of the firing chamber, which may burst. However, within this limit, high pressure is desirable as it accelerates the projectile more. Higher velocity as the projectile leaves the barrel translates to greater range, accuracy and capability to bring down a target. A longer barrel also increases muzzle velocity, as it allows the projectile to accelerate for longer. Once the projectile is out of the barrel, it is no longer being pushed by expanding gas and ceases to accelerate.

A rifled barrel spins the projectile for stability in flight, increasing range and accuracy. Bullets are aerodynamic, so stability is important to keep the nose of the projectile pointed in the right direction. If the bullet yaws in flight (waggles from side to side), it will lose energy fast as well as wandering off course. A bullet that passes through light obstructions such as leaves may become unstable in flight, but this is not usually an issue – inability to see the target will generally make a shot impossible.

A projectile does not travel in a perfectly straight line. On a long shot it may be affected by wind, and it will be pulled down by gravity. 'Bullet

Types of Bullet

Bullet configuration determines how a round behaves in the air and in the target. As a rule, a blunt round stops quickly when it hits something – and thus transfers its kinetic energy to the target efficiently – but a more pointed bullet has less air resistance and possibly superior ballistic performance.

Round nose

Semi-wadcutter

Hollow point

Wadcutter

drop' can be quite considerable over longer distances, requiring the weapon to have suitable sights for long-range fire. The arc in which a bullet travels is known as its trajectory, and it is important to consider what is above and below the target for this reason – the direct path may be clear but the bullet's trajectory might take it close to an overhead obstruction.

The amount of energy a projectile has when it leaves the barrel ('muzzle energy'), and how well it retains its

Bullet Flight

**A bullet that yaws – waggles from side
to side – in flight will not be accurate.
Spinning the round causes it to precess,
gradually cancelling out yaw in flight.
Nutation is basically a complex form of
precession, whereby the round's nose
oscillates in a complex pattern around
a central line of flight.**

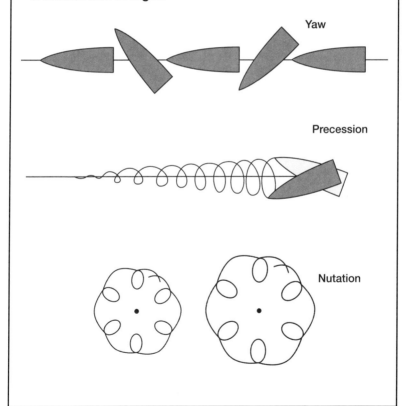

Yaw

Precession

Nutation

Rifled versus Smoothbore

A rifled barrel has grooves that grip a bullet – providing it is a tight fit – and cause it to spin. Rifling disrupts a shot pattern, however; smoothbores are far better for evenly dispersing shot.

Rifled barrel

Smoothbore barrel

energy in the face of aerodynamic friction, determines how far it will travel and how effective it will be against the target when it gets there. Muzzle energy depends on two factors: the mass of the projectile and its velocity.

A big, heavy bullet moving relatively slowly might have the same muzzle energy as a lighter round travelling faster, but it will probably shed its energy more quickly. The higher-velocity round will also have a flatter trajectory and thus be easier to aim. But velocity is not everything; projectile mass and shape are both important in determining how effective it will be against the target. A big, heavy bullet dumps its energy into the target quickly, causing more serious damage than a lighter, faster round that might tear straight through (overpenetrate) without stopping.

The Right Calibre

With all these factors to balance, the choice of weapon can be a difficult one. Long before a specific model is decided upon, the choice can be narrowed by decisions about the desired calibre of weapon. Calibre is the term for the size of projectile thrown by the weapon; for shotguns the equivalent term is 'gauge'. The calibre of a weapon is the diameter of its bore, which translates in simple terms to how big a bullet it can shoot. A larger calibre translates to a bigger bullet, but that does not necessarily

mean a better weapon. Two weapons of the same gauge or calibre will not necessarily perform identically, but they will have broadly similar characteristics and be suitable for the same tasks.

A handgun is not a good choice for your first sporting gun unless you intend to become involved in competitive target shooting, in which case you need a specialist weapon. For general 'plinking' at targets, or for range shooting, any handgun will do. A gun bought for self-defence purposes really ought to be taken to the range from time to time anyway, and range time can be part recreation, part preparation. Large-calibre pistols are sometimes used for hunting, but this is not the province of the beginner.

For shooting birds and similar small, fast-moving targets, a shotgun is the obvious choice. The most popular gauge for shotguns is 12 gauge, with 20 gauge being a lighter alternative that performs almost as well. Larger gauges are not normally seen, although the 10-gauge shotgun has recently enjoyed a resurgence in popularity. This is mainly due to the necessity of using non-toxic ammunition such as steel rather than lead shot. Since steel is less dense than lead, a slightly heavier shotgun gauge is used to compensate for the loss of power. A shotgun may be the only possible choice in some areas where other gun ownership

Resting a Rifle

Using a rest can greatly enhance accuracy. This shooter can minutely adjust his aim point by squeezing or relaxing his left hand, which will raise or lower the aim point without any lateral movement that might take the rifle off target.

Gauge

Gauge is a rather archaic measure based on the weight of the largest lead ball that will fit in a weapon's bore. The smaller the gauge number, the bigger the gun.

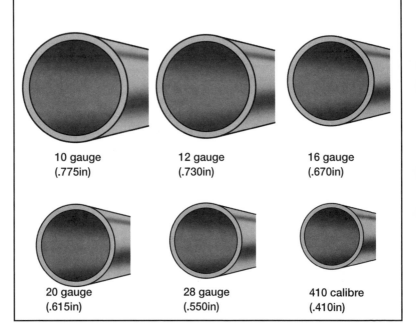

10 gauge
(.775in)

12 gauge
(.730in)

16 gauge
(.670in)

20 gauge
(.615in)

28 gauge
(.550in)

410 calibre
(.410in)

is tightly restricted by law. Smaller shotguns such as 28 gauge and .410 are primarily used for vermin control and shooting small game. Their small amount of lightweight shot makes them unsuitable for more robust targets and shortens their effective range, as well as reducing the size

of shot pattern created and therefore requiring a more accurate shot. On the plus side these light guns are easy to carry and have relatively little recoil.

For precision shooting over longer distances, a rifle is the weapon of choice. The word 'rifle' is one that has gradually changed meaning over the years. Originally it referred to any firearm that had a rifled barrel, i.e. was not smoothbore. Technically, the term could be applied to handguns and artillery pieces, but today the word 'rifle' is taken to mean a weapon used with both hands and fitted with a long, rifled barrel. A shorter and lighter example of the same general type might be termed a 'carbine' but the terms do overlap considerably.

Rifles (and carbines) generally use ammunition that is smaller in calibre than pistol rounds, but which has a longer cartridge case containing more propellant. This, along with a barrel length that permits the bullet to be accelerated for longer, creates a flatter trajectory and shorter flight time than a typical shotgun or handgun. A short flight time means that the target has less time to move between the shot being fired and the round arriving, and reduces the effects of wind. However, rifles are generally used for longer-range shooting than other weapons, so velocity is offset to some extent by increased distance.

Rifles can be subdivided, in general, into 'smallbore' and 'fullbore' types. The terms are not universally used, but they provide a reasonable distinction. Smallbore weapons are typically in the .22, .223 or 5.56x45mm range (the same class as most military assault rifles). Smallbore rifles are not suitable for very long-range shooting or tackling large game, but are otherwise versatile and generally lightweight. That can be important during a long day shooting in the wilderness.

Fullbore rifles use a larger, more powerful cartridge. In the UK, most fullbore shooting uses 7.62x51mm weapons, the same calibre as many military sniper weapons and 'battle rifles'. Other calibres in the same range fall into the fullbore category. Weapons of this sort are useful for longer-range shooting and for tackling large targets such as deer or dangerous game. Fullbore ammunition is heavier and more expensive than smallbore.

Fit for Purpose

As with other weapons, the choice of rifle depends on what you intend doing with it. For a bit of fun target practice, a very small calibre gun such as a .22LR will be fine; these guns are suitable for younger shooters who cannot handle a larger weapon, and can serve admirably as varmint guns or for hunting small game.

If you intend shooting over any great distance, or tracking large creatures such as deer, a fullbore rifle is probably the best choice. Extremely powerful weapons are available for specialist purposes such as hunting dangerous game, but these would obviously not be the first choice of most shooters for more general use.

Cleaning Kit

A good gun-cleaning kit should contain everything you need to keep the weapon in working order. The phosphor bronze brushes are especially useful for cleaning off stubborn propellant and lead deposits from inside the gun's barrel.

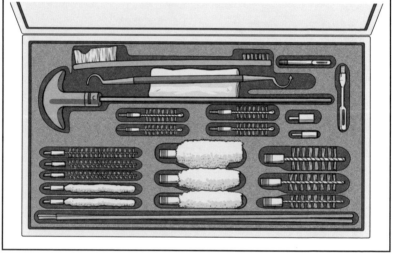

Combination guns do exist, with two breech-loading barrels in either an over-under configuration or side by side. The combination of a shotgun and a rifle does allow some flexibility when the shooter does not know what game he will encounter next, but a certain amount of experience is necessary to make the selection quickly enough to be able to take the shot. Such weapons are expensive and only useful to a small proportion of shooters.

Buying a gun is not something that should be rushed into. Within the same price bracket the quality of weapons can vary considerably, and what might seem like minor differences in design can make one gun virtually unusable to a given shooter while another is perfect. Thus it is worth remembering that one decent gun will probably cost you less than a cheap one and a better replacement. It might be worth putting off buying your own guns until you are sure of what you want and have the skills to make best use of them.

Top-end sporting guns can cost a fabulous amount of money; over a hundred thousand dollars is not uncommon for a prestige weapon from a famous manufacturer. Fortunately, it is possible to get a serviceable gun for a few hundred dollars and a really very good one for a couple of thousand. At the top end you are paying for the name and the craftsmanship that goes into creating the firearm rather than its ability to shoot straight, although at that price excellent performance should be a given.

It is not necessary to spend a vast fortune on your sporting gun, but to some extent you do get what you pay for, as some cheap guns are not well made and may not shoot as accurately as you might like. That matters a lot to an expert, but a beginner might not be skilled enough to tell whether a miss was due to faulty technique or a poor gun. It takes a lot of practice to get to the point where you can outshoot even a fairly cheap gun, but once you get there then the weapon will be a limiting factor.

Maintenance

Maintenance is something that should be considered before you buy a gun. Most sporting guns are not excessively complicated, and the majority are designed to be rugged. That does not mean that maintenance and cleaning can be neglected of course, but it does mean that most guns are fairly simple to look after. You are unlikely to render your weapon unusable by simply

Safety Catch

It is a matter of common sense that the safety catch should be on at any time you are not immediately intending to shoot. The only time it should be off with a round chambered is when you are waiting for a target that you expect to appear. Forgetting to take the safety off is embarrassing and will cause you to miss a shot, but it's better than the alternative.

Hunting Rifle Kit

A hunter's rifle kit can include many accessories, such as cleaning kit, data log, ballistic calculator and cheek pads.

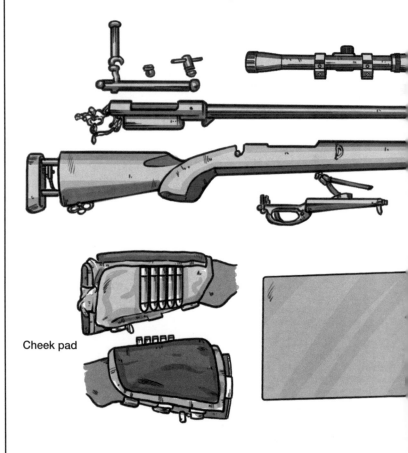

Cheek pad

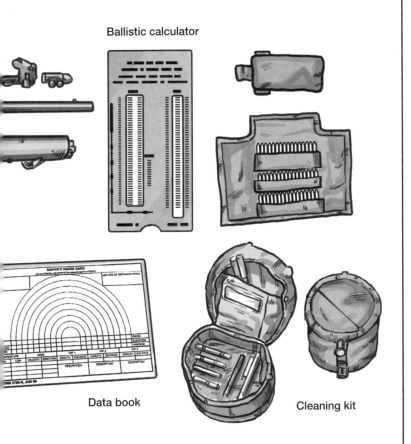

Ballistic calculator

Data book

Cleaning kit

stripping it down to clean it. However, it is worth getting some instruction in firearms maintenance when you buy your first gun.

Maintenance is essential to keeping weapons in good condition. One that fails to fire or to feed ammunition because the mechanism is dirty is mostly an embarrassment to the user, although it can leave him with a weapon that might go off if knocked, or a jammed round that cannot be easily removed. Poor maintenance can cause more serious problems, such as malfunctions that result in an accidental discharge. Worn components can cause the safety catch to fail to function, for example, or can make a trigger much easier to operate, creating a 'hair trigger' situation where the weapon might discharge long before the user expects it to.

Firearms propel their projectiles using what amounts to a small explosion in the breech, which creates a great deal of hot gas. This normally has nowhere to go, so pushes the projectile down the barrel. However, the chamber pressure can be very high and this can cause a badly maintained weapon to be damaged; it can even burst the firing chamber, throwing hot metal fragments around. This is extremely dangerous, since the chamber is usually in close proximity to the user's head and hands.

Shooters should be competent enough to conduct simple routine maintenance on their weapon, but modifications should be made by a qualified gunsmith unless the user is very experienced. Some modifications may make a weapon illegal, but this is perhaps less serious than one that causes the weapon to malfunction when firing. In any case, quality sporting guns are expensive and should not be interfered with by the non-expert, so it is well worth learning how to take care of your weapon properly. It is always best to seek advice about a problem that you are not confident to tackle.

Pistols

Some hunters carry a handgun for self-defence in case something goes horribly wrong on a shooting trip. This is not a sporting application, and in many cases the weapon chosen is a 'combat handgun' rather than a sporting gun. A gun carried for self-defence will be selected using different criteria to one for sporting purposes. However, 'kit guns' or 'camp guns' are sometimes carried for the dual purpose of self-defence and shooting small game.

Kit Guns

Most kit guns are lightweight weapons chambered for small calibres such as .22LR. Often kept loaded with shotshells for dealing with snakes, kit guns can also be used to shoot small game such as rabbits. Against dangerous wildlife

Air Pistol

Some target-shooting disciplines use air pistols rather than conventional firearms. The technique is more or less the same.

Types of Sporting Pistols

Top-end target pistol shooting uses weapons that only vaguely resemble combat handguns. They are designed for the sole purpose of putting a round exactly where the user wants it.

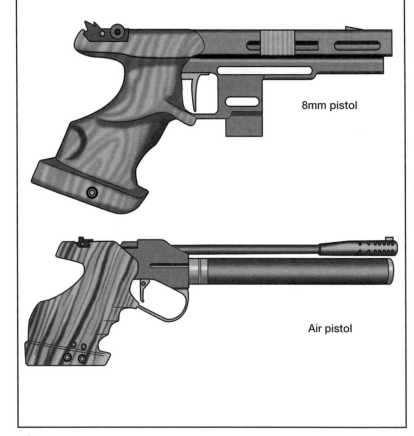

8mm pistol

Air pistol

such as a bear, a small-calibre gun of this sort is pretty much useless.

A kit gun needs to be robust and reliable. It may spend much of its life in a tackle box or in among an assortment of tools and equipment in a bag. Even if carried in a holster, a kit gun is going to be lugged over rough ground and through environments as unfavourable to machinery as they are to humans. It also must be highly accurate and easy to shoot with, as it will be used to shoot small targets such as rabbits.

Larger-calibre weapons can be carried as kit guns, but their powerful cartridges represent overkill when used to take small game, whereas the light weight and recoil of a very small-calibre weapon may well make it much more suitable. Small-calibre ammunition tends to be cheap, which is a consideration if you intend to use your gun to shoot dinner or to keep down pests.

A wide variety of handguns are used for 'plinking' or fun target shooting. Any handgun will do for this purpose, although obviously a quality gun will be more accurate and thus more satisfying for a skilled user.

Target Pistol Shooting

Competitive target pistol shooting is a wholly different field to plinking for fun. It is a serious business, and the weapons used can be very specialized. There are competitions in which conventional revolvers and semi-automatics can be used, but many events use specialist target weapons that scarcely resemble a handgun intended for combat. With grips made specially for the user's hand, extremely light trigger pull and a very long barrel, these weapons are used in some very demanding events, including shooting at 50m (164ft) range with the weapon held in one hand only. This is an extremely specialized skillset.

Specialist target shooting weapons are extremely expensive and require careful looking after. They could in theory be used to take small game, but many target guns are temperamental creatures that would protest at being mistreated in this way. A gun that will go out of kilter as soon as it is exposed to the rugged conditions of field shooting should be reserved for the rarefied atmosphere of the formal competition and not asked to work for a living.

Thus top-end target pistol shooting is a very specialist arena that is distinct from other shooting sports. However, there are competitive events that are suited to more modest and multipurpose handguns. 'Practical pistol' events are a form of target shooting based on self-defence scenarios. The weapons of choice are combat handguns, and factors such as ease of reloading and speed of handling at close range are more important than long-range accuracy.

Hunting Handgun

The single-shot hunting handgun uses a robust falling-block action to take the heavy cartridges needed for killing large prey.

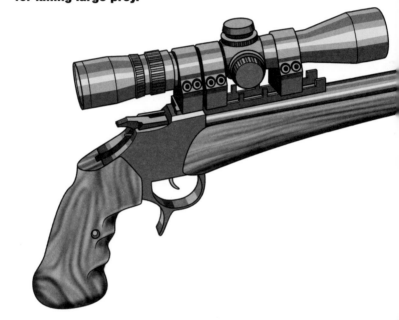

Straight target shooting, i.e. competitive range shooting, can be undertaken with any handgun, although obviously a good-quality gun will produce better results in the hands of a skilled shooter. Smaller-calibre ammunition is cheaper than more potent rounds, which may not be very important in a competition, but when you factor in the amount of practice required to stand a chance in competition, ammunition costs become very significant.

The guns used for target shooting tend to be high-quality versions of standard combat handguns, at

If conventional handguns are used for these events, they tend to be fitted with a telescopic sight and have an extremely long barrel. Shooting is normally from a rest but some competitions require the weapon to be held in the hand. A range of unusual firing positions have been developed for these events.

Hunting with Handguns

Hunting with handguns is extremely challenging, mainly because it is difficult to shoot accurately at any great distance with a pistol. Where conventional handguns are used, these tend to be long-barrelled weapons with a telescopic sight fitted. Calibres range from .22LR suitable for small game all the way up to extremely powerful rounds that can bring down a deer or other large game if an accurate shot can be made. The most extreme of these include weapons chambered for .50 calibre bullets, which will stop a Cape buffalo. The recoil generated by such monster rounds is not for the inexperienced or faint-hearted shooter.

Specialist hunting handguns are available, often single-shot weapons firing a rifle-calibre round. These often resemble a cut-down rifle fitted with a pistol grip and use bolt action or a break-open reloading system rather than more conventional handgun operation. There are even models that have a built-in bipod. These weapons

least up to a point. More specialized events such as long-range shooting usually require specialist weapons. The more extreme long-range events involve shooting at 500m (1640ft) or even 1000m (3280ft) with a handgun – ranges that are beyond the capability of many rifle shooters.

Unusual Firearm Types

While bolt-action rifles all tend to come in a recognizable format, semi-automatic rifles have some more outlandish specimens. Many of these are civilian versions of military weapons. The Barrett M82A1, for example, is a .50 BMG semi-automatic recoil-operated sniper rifle, its massive box magazine holding 10 of the huge rounds. The Bushmaster XM15 rifles and several other similar weapon makes are effectively U.S. military M16 assault rifles without the full-automatic facility and some of the military fitment.

Military-style semi-automatic guns have to be treated with caution, because, when used in hunting formats, they can give shooters a bad press. This is especially the case if the shooter goes over the top when accessorizing – a 30-round magazine of 7.62mm ammunition just isn't necessary on a hunting trip when you might see only a single deer, if you're lucky. However, in growing sports such as practical shooting, or for long-range target shooting or home defence, they have their place.

Prices of semi-automatic rifles vary widely from a couple of hundred dollars for a cheap rimfire through to the $7000 needed to buy a new Barrett. As always, the rule is buy the best quality of gun you can for the exact purpose that you require.

are not quite handguns in the usual sense, but they are not rifles either. Since they increase the challenge they are more likely to be used for recreational hunting than 'serious' shooting such as wildlife culls or hunting for the table, although there are some who like the light weight and ease of carry that comes with a hunting pistol. The choice of hunting pistol is largely determined by the intended target. As already noted, a small-calibre camp gun is entirely sufficient to take small game, but for larger targets, a heavier round is needed. Small-calibre hunting pistols are often semi-automatics, but larger weapons shooting .357 Magnum, .44 Magnum and other heavy rounds tend to be revolvers. Semi-automatics chambered for these calibres are available but they tend to be very expensive.

A long-barrelled revolver might be too heavy and unwieldy for self-defence purposes and might even be a liability for home defence. The weapon's size might be a drawback inside a building. However, these handguns are about as well suited to hunting as any non-longarm. A long barrel improves accuracy and increases muzzle velocity, which can be important when trying to take down large game, but there is a limit to how accurate a handgun can be, even with a scope.

Handgun ammunition also does not penetrate as well as higher-velocity, smaller-diameter rounds such as rifle ammunition. Some large game animals are extremely robust, and a handgun round needs to be very potent in order to penetrate to the vital organs and ensure a quick kill – or indeed any sort of kill. A wounded animal will suffer a lot more than one that is instantly disabled, so anyone hunting with a handgun has a responsibility to ensure he only shoots what his gun can realistically kill.

Although not specifically for hunting, large-calibre handguns are sometimes a good backup when camping or hunting in bear country. While hunting bear with a short-barrelled .44 Magnum revolver would be an exercise in idiocy, a powerful backup gun may be a life-saver if a bear invades your camp or a wounded animal rushes the shooter instead of fleeing.

Rifles

If the subject of shotgun choice can provoke debate among experts, that of rifle choice can be even more vigorous. Hunting rifles come in numerous shapes, sizes and calibres, from small-bore guns only suited to shooting squirrels up to shoulder-pounding weapons that can drop an elephant.

For most hunters, the ideal type of weapon to take into the field is the bolt-action rifle. Bolt-action rifles are generally rugged, reliable and outstandingly accurate, delivering precision kills (depending on the calibre) from a couple of hundred metres to distances of more than a mile. Although bolt-action mechanisms vary in construction from gun to gun, with significant differences in such features as the number of locking lugs, type of extractor, method of feed (either magazine or single shot) and build quality, all mechanisms perform the same job – a hand-operated bolt system loads, fires and ejects the cartridge.

Semi-automatics

An alternative to the bolt-action rifle is the semi-automatic rifle. A semi-auto rifle is a magazine-fed weapon

U.S. Army Tip – Problems with Weapons in Cold Weather

Sluggishness – normal lubricants thicken in low temperature, and stoppage or sluggish action of firearms results. During the winter, weapons must be stripped completely and cleaned with a dry cleaning solvent to remove all lubricants and rust prevention compounds. These lubricants will provide proper lubrication during the winter and help minimize snow and ice from freezing on the weapons.

Breakages and Malfunctions – these can also be attributed primarily to the cold, although snow in a weapon may cause

in which a round is loaded, fired and its casing ejected automatically with every pull of the trigger. Semi-automatic rifles are not available to the citizens of every country – they are prohibited in the UK, for instance – but they offer ultra-quick follow-up shots with no change in the shooter's body position. This is in contrast to the bolt-action gun, where the shooter has to perform a manual reloading action that can alert prey to his presence; the action might also force a change in body position.

Semi-automatics have a mixed press as hunting weapons. The auto-loading mechanism of a semi-

stoppage and malfunctions. One of the main problems is to insure that snow and ice do not get into the working parts, sights or barrel. The weapon must be carefully handled during movement through the snow-covered woods, and especially under combat conditions in deep snow.

Condensation – this forms on weapons when they are taken from the extreme cold into any type of heated shelter. This condensation is often referred to as 'sweating'. When weapons are taken into heated shelter for cleaning purposes, 'sweating' may continue for as long as an hour. Therefore, when time is available, wait one hour, remove all condensation and then clean the weapon.

– FM 31-70, *Basic Cold Weather* Manual, Appendix D

auto rifle doesn't generally seat the cartridge in the chamber as consistently as a bolt-action gun, hence it is less accurate over long ranges than the manually operated weapon. (For practical purposes, the differences in accuracy tend to be negligible at ranges of up to 300m/984ft.) The semi-auto might also promote, in undisciplined shooters, a tendency to rely upon firepower rather than accuracy to achieve a kill.

Such is especially the case when assault-type rifles, with large magazine capacities, are used for hunting. It is far better to achieve a one-hit kill with a single shot.

Lever-action Mechanism

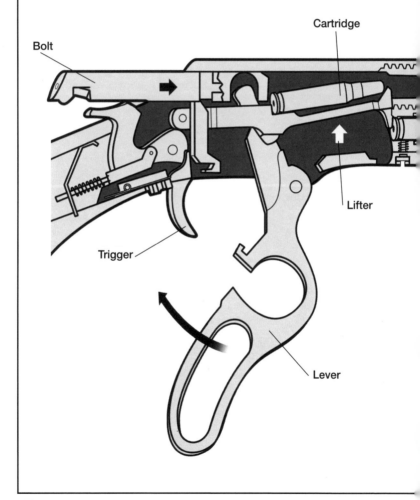

Cartridge

Bolt

Lifter

Trigger

Lever

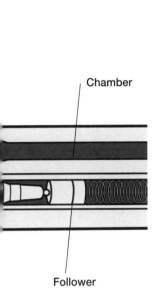

Chamber

Follower

Lever-action weapons are best suited to shooting from a standing or kneeling position. The need to move the trigger guard assembly downward can be problematical when trying to shoot from a prone position.

Given these reservations, the semi-auto does at least offer you a quick follow-up shot on a wounded animal, reducing the prospect of its disappearing into the bush.

Lever-action Rifles

Another, rather traditional option for rifle configuration is the lever action, most famously embodied in the Winchester/Henry series of rifles that dominated the American West. A lever-action gun usually feeds from a tubular under-barrel magazine, the cycle of loading, firing and ejection performed by operating a lever that forms an integral part of the trigger guard.

Lever-action guns are quick to fire and reliable in operation, and they remain very popular with hunters worldwide. In terms of disadvantages, they are often limited in the types of pointed ammunition they can use, as the bullet of one round rests against the primer of the round in front in the magazine, running the risk of an accidental cartridge discharge. (There are some specialist ammunition types that now negate this problem successfully.)

For this reason, lever-action guns are often used for short/medium-range shooting with lighter calibres, although there are lever guns on the market specifically designed for heavier game. Note that, like the bolt action, the lever action can

Lever-action Rifles

Lever-action rifles remain popular among hunters, not least for their ability to provide a quick follow-up shot if necessary. They tend to be short and handy, which is useful in woods and other cluttered terrain.

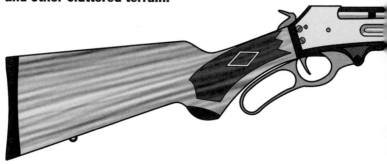

be awkward to operate in certain positions, particularly if the shooter is lying prone.

A final category of hunting rifle is the breech-loading rifle, this being loaded in the same manner as a break-barrel shotgun. These rifles tend to be at the large-calibre end of the spectrum, and hence are used for big game shooting. If you venture into this territory, make sure that you receive proper training before using the gun in earnest – the power of such weapons needs to be tamed by good technique if you are to avoid injury.

Airguns

Airguns are the most easily accessible of hunting weapons. Even in countries with very restrictive firearms licensing regulations, such as the UK, airguns are usually available to purchase without any legal restriction by an adult. (In some countries, such as the UK, if air weapons exceed a certain level of power and muzzle velocity, they might fall within restrictions placed upon powder firearms – check government statutes for details.)

Air pistols, contrary to what anyone might say, should never be used for hunting purposes, as

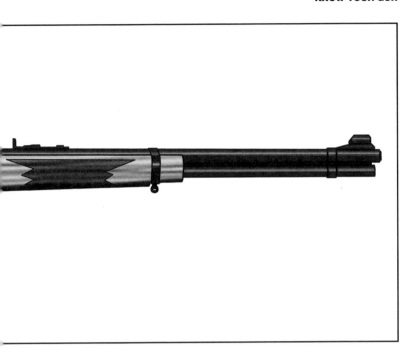

they have neither the power nor the accuracy for the job. Air rifles, by contrast, are well suited to hunting small or medium-sized birds and game. The most common calibres are .177 and .22, and there are pros and cons to each. The .22 – the most popular in a hunting context – has a greater surface area and so imparts a better impact on the target. The lighter .177, by contrast, delivers less punch but it achieves higher muzzle velocities for the same power, and so delivers a flatter trajectory and greater accuracy. As a general rule, the .177 is fine for small birds and pest

control, but the .22 should be used for rabbiting and on other similarly sized game.

Note that all air rifles have range limitations, however, by virtue of the low mass of an air pellet. A typical air rifle will have an effective range of 30–50m (98–165ft), with the most powerful models exceeding 100m (328ft). Make sure you are using appropriate hunting pellets – standard flat- or dome-headed target pellets will be fine for small creatures like rats, but for rabbits and larger birds, choose pointed-tip pellets with better penetration. (Put padding in your

Spring Gun

Many air rifles use a break action to both expose the breech for loading and to ready the weapon by cocking the spring. When released, it snaps forward, creating high air pressure in the breech and launching the pellet on its way.

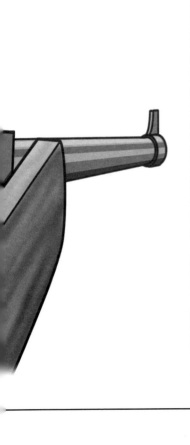

pellet tin, as damaged points will affect the efficient flight of the pellets.)

When it comes to choosing an air rifle, the range of options available is vast. You can make a useful subdivision into hand-cocked rifles or pre-charged rifles. Hand-cocked rifles are, as their name suggests, weapons that require manually cocking before a pellet can be fired. This action is typically performed by either 'breaking' the entire barrel downwards, at the point where the barrel meets the action, or by a charging lever running alongside or underneath the barrel. In both actions the procedure cocks a spring-loaded piston in a compression chamber. Pulling the trigger releases the piston, compressing the air behind the pellet (loaded into the bore port at the end of the barrel); the air pressure builds up to the extent that the pellet overcomes its inertia in the bore chamber and is forced explosively down the barrel to begin its flight.

Spring Guns
The advantage of 'break-barrel' weapons is that they are typically rather inexpensive compared to other types of air rifle, but they are also robust and reliable, as numerous generations of schoolchildren have discovered in their back gardens. They deliver serviceable accuracy, but the fact that the barrel is movable compromises accuracy over long ranges. Side- or under-barrel lever

guns get around this problem by having a fixed barrel, the cocking performed by a separate mechanism.

These air rifles, especially in their more expensive incarnations, are very good hunting weapons, although in their heart they are still 'spring guns'. Disadvantages of such firearms are that the shifting mass of the compression piston can affect accuracy at the point of firing, and the 'lock time' (the interval between pulling the trigger and the pellet being fired) can also be longer than desirable, again with a negative impact on accuracy. Spring guns tend to be on the noisier side of air rifle volume, and the cocking action might be a problem if a hunter wants to remain inconspicuous while reloading for another shot.

The term 'pre-charged' is actually shorthand for a range of air rifles, the details of which are too technical to go into at any length here. In essence, however, these air rifles store gas (CO_2) or air in a cylinder, filled prior to using the weapon. The cylinder contains enough gas for multiple shots – up to 500 in advanced models – and once the cylinder is expended, it needs recharging. This process is performed from assorted means and sources, including diver's air bottle, CO_2 canister or manual pump.

Compared to the spring guns, pre-charged air rifles are usually expensive, but they deliver

exceptional performance for the extra money. They are outstandingly accurate over their effective range, and many models have multi-shot magazines, meaning that the gun doesn't require full reloading after each shot. They are hyper quiet – a hunter can take out one animal without unduly disturbing others in the vicinity. Pre-charged guns can also deliver a performance that rivals some small-calibre propellant weapons.

A good air rifle is doubtless a valuable item for any hunter to have in his arsenal. Yet the fact remains that for anything over the size of a rabbit, or moving or at any distance, a hunter requires the undeniable force of powder and bullet.

Bolt-action Rifles

Bolt-action rifles are the world's most popular firearms purchases. While the shotgun is the ideal gun for hunting small ground animals and birds at ranges of up to 50m (164ft), the rifle can take on far larger prey at much longer distances, with an accuracy within mere millimetres or centimetres of the point of aim. Although bolt-action mechanisms vary in construction from gun to gun, with differences in such features as number of locking lugs, type of extractor, method of feed and overall build quality, all mechanisms perform the same job – a hand-operated bolt system loads, locks, fires and ejects

Bolt-action Mechanism

The bolt-action mechanism is simple and robust, and easy to use in most positions. The action is worked with the firing hand, allowing the fore hand to keep the weapon on target.

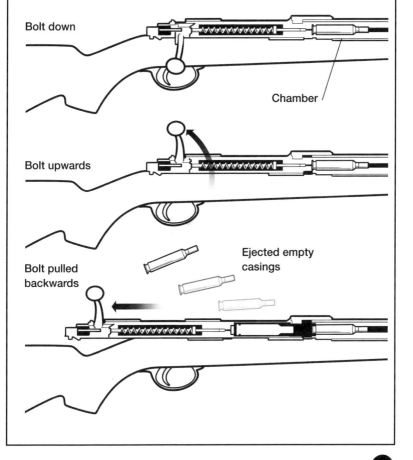

Bolt down

Chamber

Bolt upwards

Bolt pulled backwards

Ejected empty casings

Calibres

Rifle bullets are more or less the same in configuration, but vary considerably in size. A larger round will go further and penetrate more, which may not always be an advantage.

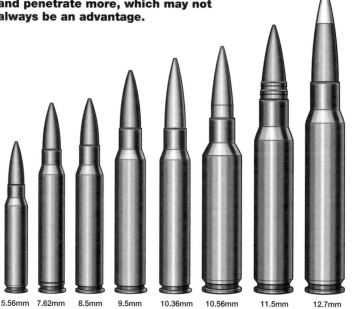

| 5.56mm | 7.62mm | 8.5mm | 9.5mm | 10.36mm | 10.56mm | 11.5mm | 12.7mm |

the cartridge. In a lever-action gun, the rounds are pumped in from a tubular magazine via a lever set as part of the trigger guard. The big difference between rifles, however, tends to lie in calibre.

Choice of Calibre

The range of calibres available for

rifles is truly vast. At the small end of the scale are the popular rimfire calibres, such as .22 Short (S), Long (L) and Long Rifle (LR). A .22LR, one of the most popular rounds for bolt- and lever-action guns, has a bullet weight of below 40 grains, a muzzle velocity of around 320m/ sec (1050ft/sec) and is useful for

of up to and beyond 100m/328ft.) For deer shooting, use a centrefire round. Such cartridges are larger and therefore generate more powerful muzzle velocities and kinetic energy. Opinion varies on the entry-level calibre, but between .240 and .338 is a good bracket. Beyond this are the big-game calibres referred to earlier. These start with rounds like the .358 Norma Magnum and run up to the .600 Nitro (a 900-grain bullet), and are designed for the very largest animals, such as antelope, bear (although many of the deer calibres will handle these creatures at the appropriate range) and safari creatures. This run-through of the calibre selections available is very simplistic, and space does not allow a full consideration. Get expert consultation when buying a rifle, find the right calibre and make sure that you can handle both gun and calibre well.

Good Shooting

In this chapter we only consider the rifle, paying attention to sights purely in terms of whether the gun has open sights and/or what provision there is for scope mounting. A rifle, however, is only as accurate as its sight. There are three basic types of sight: open, aperture and telescopic. Open sights are the least accurate but, generally speaking, the quickest to use. They tend to appeal to close-quarters woodland hunters, who might see a flash of prey through the trees and need to make a snap shot at ranges seldom more than 50m (164ft). Anything beyond this range will generally need a more advanced sighting system.

Aperture sights are usually found on target rifles, and they give very accurate performance out to and beyond 100m (328ft). Yet as the small rear aperture sight has limited light transmission, they are rarely used on hunting weapons. Hunting rifles generally need telescopic sights. These come in numerous varieties and capabilities, but will give the shooter range capabilities that can comfortably stretch over several hundred metres.

Of course, a good sight is also meaningless unless it is zeroed properly. This takes practice and training, as do all aspects of rifle shooting. Don't fall into the trap of thinking that a good sight is all that it takes to be a competent rifle shot. Rifle shooting, like all other forms of shooting, is an advanced practice and incorporates everything from fieldcraft to a decent understanding of ballistics. Strive to be a complete shooter and you will discover much more about the passion of rifle shooting.

Semi-automatic Rifles

The citizens of many countries, including the United States (within a state-variable and complex history

Walther G22

The G22 is a bullpup-configuration weapon, i.e. its magazine is inserted behind the trigger assembly. This creates a very short weapon that can still have quite a long barrel.

small game such as rabbits, foxes and gophers at ranges of around 50m (164ft). At the absolute other extreme, a big-game centrefire cartridge, such as the massive .460 Weatherby Magnum, has a bullet weight of 500 grains, a muzzle velocity of 823m/sec (2700ft/sec) and could bring down a bull elephant at 500m (1640ft). The LAR Grizzly rifle fires a .50 BMG round that, in military use, has made kills well beyond

2000m (6561ft). The important point is that you select a calibre of rifle appropriate to its intended use. For plinking, target shooting or small-game hunting, opt for a rimfire weapon in .17 or .22 calibre. (Be careful, however, of high-velocity rimfires such as the .17 HMR or .22 WRF Magnum. The velocity of these rounds will destroy a small animal at close range, and they are therefore better suited to ranges

of legislation), can own a magazine-fed rifle that automatically loads the next round after a shot is fired. However, in many other countries these firearms are often classified as assault rifles, and are therefore banned from the hands of anyone but a soldier or police officer.

For example, the 1987 massacre of 16 people in the English town of Hungerford by Michael Ryan, who was armed with an AK47,

led the British Government to ban the ownership of centrefire semi-automatic rifles. Furthermore, many countries (and certain U.S. states) prohibit the use of semi-automatic rifles for deer hunting or similar types of hunting.

The second factor in the relatively small number of semi-automatic rifles bought is the common perception (not necessarily always accurate) that a semi-automatic rifle

Ruger Mini 14

The Ruger Mini 14 is a centrefire rifle chambered for the .223 Rem (5.56mm) cartridge. It belongs to Ruger's 'Ranch Rifle' series of auto-loaders, giving a suggestion of its suitable usage. The .223 Rem is high-velocity round that is also currently the NATO standard calibre for its assault rifles and small arms. Muzzle velocity for a 55-grain bullet is around 975m/sec (3200ft/sec), and with the proper grade of ammunition and the right scope, accurate shots can be taken out to several hundred metres. However, the .223 is not a deep-penetrating round – it tends to fragment on impact – so it is ideally used for varmint hunting and not on larger prey (although some authorities, not without controversy, feel that the round is appropriate for small deer).

The Mini 14 is a compact .223 Rem autoloader retailing for up to around $800. It has a 47cm (18.5in) barrel and, being a centrefire weapon, is cycled via a fixed-piston gas mechanism. The breech bolt locking system is based on the legendary Garand rifle, so reliable function is rarely disturbed in the Mini 14.

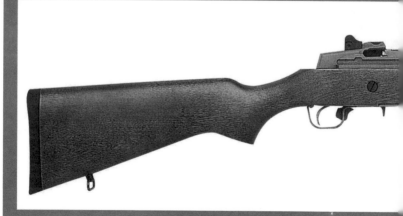

The Ranch Rifle series is, in Ruger's words, 'specifically designed for mounting today's scopes or other optical sighting systems'. This is achieved by setting the scope bases directly into the receiver, hence ensuring that they 'can never shoot loose'. The side-ejection system is also set to prevent empty shell interference with the scope, and Ruger also points in its publicity to its 'patented recoil buffer, which protects the scope from damage or shifting impact when the mechanism parts move automatically during firing'. Beyond the scope fittings, however, Ghost Ring aperture sights are also fitted.

Specifications: Ruger Mini 14
Calibre: .223 Rem
Barrel length: 47cm (18.5in)
Weight: 2.9kg (6.4lb)
Sights: integral scope bases; Ghost Ring aperture sights
Mechanism: gas operated

does not offer the hunting accuracy of a bolt-action weapon. The debate is ongoing, but it should be kept in mind that there are a good number of semi-automatic police and military-sniper rifles out there, all calibrated for the greatest demands on accuracy.

Rimfire/Centrefire

So what is the position of the semi-automatic rifle today? Calibre can be an indication. A great many semi-automatic rifles are small-calibre rimfire weapons. These often use a blowback mechanism (the bolt and barrel are not locked together, the pressure of the firing gases on the cartridge pushing back the bolt to cycle the weapon) and are cheap to produce. Rimfires are generally used for plinking, target shooting, small-game hunting and, indeed, any form of shooting that can use up plenty of cartridges at relatively short ranges.

Having a semi-automatic firearm means that the hunter can, for example, take on a colony of rabbits without having to crank a bolt handle between each shot and further alert the targets.

Yet even on larger game the semi-automatic can have a place. Centrefire semi-automatics tend almost always to be gas-operated firearms. The gas system absorbs much of the recoil generated by the powerful centrefire cartridges, and so

makes for more controllable multiple shots. All shooters have in their time only wounded an animal with their first shot, and having a rapid follow-up shot can reduce the chance of the animal escaping wounded into the undergrowth. Good-quality semi-automatics, such as the Benelli R1, control the recoil to such an extent that an aimed follow-up shot can be taken within a second of the first round being fired.

The key word here is 'aimed'. Semi-automatics in themselves are fine hunting weapons; the main problem with them is that they can be both dangerous and unsporting in the wrong hands. As long as the hunter exercises self-control, is well trained and takes care that he or she only pulls the trigger when the aim is good and the picture of the target is clear, then the fire capabilities of the gun do not really matter. If, however, the shooter sprays fire in the general direction of a target, hoping for at least one terminal strike, that is unacceptable.

When firing a semi-automatic rifle, keep a keen awareness of your backdrop at all times. While your first shot's overflight might go safely into a bank of earth, if taken quickly on the swing, the second shot might inadvertently be taken when there is nothing but clear blue sky behind the target. Use the semi-automatic rifle with the same disciplined mentality as a single-shot gun, and

Open Sights

Various forms of open sights exist, but the principle is the same. Lining up the rear notch and the front blade ensures that the weapon is correctly aligned, and placing the front sight over the target should result in a hit.

Guns with Scopes

Telescopic sights ('scopes') are primarily used with rifles – many rifles come with a scope as standard – but a low-powered scope might be useful with a shotgun, primarily when hunting with solid slug rounds.

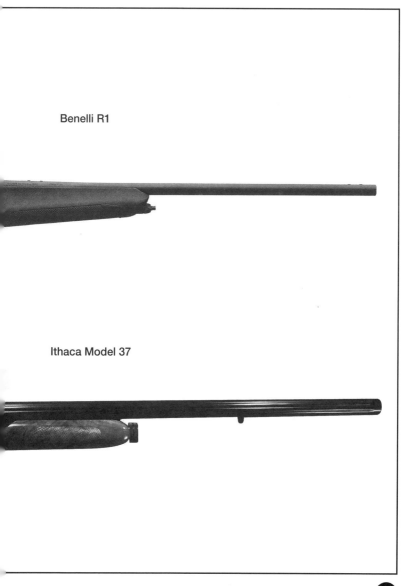

Benelli R1

Ithaca Model 37

High-powered Rifles

any arguments against its use should disappear.

Shotguns

Shotguns are smoothbore firearms with a unique type of ammunition. Instead of delivering a single projectile to a precise point, shotguns fire multiple pellets from a single cartridge, the pellets spreading to form a lethal cone-shape in the air. Because the spread of the shot compensates for a lack of precise accuracy, shotguns are superb weapons for engaging fast-moving or flying prey. (Note, however, that many people unfamiliar with shotgunning overestimate how much the shot spread will compensate for poor technique, and are shocked by how hard it can be to hit anything.) Shotgunning is, therefore, a unique form of shooting. The skilled shotgunner must understand the principle of

High-powered rifles are primarily used for long-distance shooting or taking down large or dangerous game. They require some training to use properly, and are not a good choice for beginning shooters.

'lead' perfectly – firing at the point where the target will be when the shot arrives, and not at the target's visible presence. Shotguns can be divided into three basic types:

- Break barrel
- Pump-action (also known as 'slide guns')
- Semi-automatic

Break-barrel guns are the classic shotgun type, loaded by opening a hinged barrel and inserting a cartridge directly into the chamber(s) before closing the barrel for firing. Most break-barrel guns are double-barrel types, the two barrels set in either an over-and-under or side-by-side configuration, giving the hunter two available shots before reloading. After the gun is fired, opening it results in either the empty cartridges being raised up for manual extraction or thrown clear of the gun by mechanical ejection.

Baikal IZH-27/Remington SPR-310

Baikal/Izhevsky Mekhanichesky Zavod introduced the IZH-27/SPR-310 in 1973. It is a basic over-and-under double-barrel shotgun, available in many gauges, including 12, 16, 20, 28 and .410. These budget weapons can often have a rudimentary quality of barrel blacking and finish, but their reliability and performance are not in doubt. Barrel bores and chambers are all lined with chromium to ward off corrosion from either weather or propellants, and the locking mechanism meets international guidelines for strength. (Indeed, Baikal shotguns are known for their near-indestructible qualities.) Safety is also a primary feature, with the safety mechanism locking the sears while hammer interceptors provide more reassurance.

The SPR-310 has several variant types, differences between the models centering on cartridge-extraction and barrel-selection features. Chokes are of the interchangeable variety on the 12-,

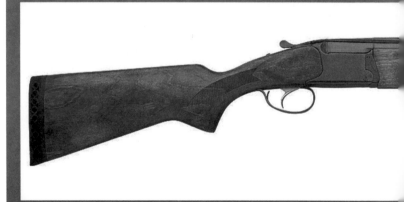

16- and 20-gauge guns, with the 28 gauge and .410 having fixed chokes. The 28 typically has Improved cylinder and Modified chokes, while the .410 has Improved, Modified and Full. Remington has also brought out the SPR-310S Sporting model, designed specifically for the clay-shooting market. This not only comes with screw-in multichokes, but it also has sophisticated features such as a ported barrel (to reduce muzzle flip) and a palm swell on the right side of the pistol grip.

Specifications: Remington SPR-310
Gauge/calibre: 12, 16, 20, 28, .410
Barrel length: 66cm (26in), 71cm (28in)
Weight: 3.4kg (7.5lb)
Ejector type: automatic ejectors
Chokes: fixed or interchangeable depending on model

Double-barrelled Shotgun

A decent over-under shotgun is a good choice for many applications. The gun can be adjusted to fit the user by altering the comb (cheek rest) and varying the thickness of the recoil pad.

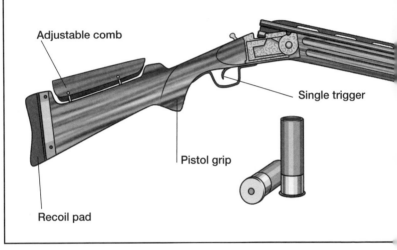

Adjustable comb

Single trigger

Pistol grip

Recoil pad

Break-barrel double shotguns are ubiquitous hunting weapons, and have been for well over a century. The much-debated argument over the relative superiority of over-and-under against side-by-side ultimately boils down to personal preference; although over-and-under configurations are the best sellers, the same results can be obtained in experienced hands with a good side-by-side. What is truly important is that you have the gun fitted to your body size, which can be done by an experienced gun seller. When the gun is mounted in your shoulder, and your cheek is sat on the upper part of the stock, you should be able to see a few millimetres visual depth of the rib that extends along the top of the barrel.

If you are instead looking into the back of the action, or the rib looks like a ski ramp, then the gun isn't

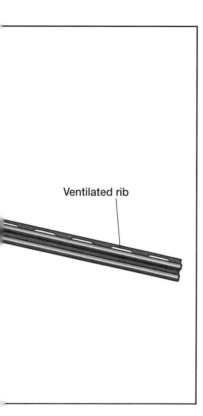

Ventilated rib

going to shoot where you look, and your hunting experience can be a very frustrating one.

Breech-loading Shotguns

For those wanting to buy a breech-loading shotgun, the choice is initially bewildering. The majority of shotguns are either side-by-sides (where the barrels are side-by-side) or over-and-unders, so choosing between the two formats is often the first, and

simplest, decision. Side-by-sides tend to be light, have a very different sight plane to over-and-unders (which are flatter, with the rib set only a short distance from the front hand), recoil in a lateral manner, and also, many feel, bring with them the older traditions and aesthetics of shotgunning.

Over-and-unders, by stacking the barrels on top of one another, give a much slimmer view down the barrel, recoil straight in line with the shoulder, interfere less with the peripheral vision and, generally, seem to take the lion's share of innovation. (The over-and-under's recoil makes it better for rapid shooting, hence it is almost universally standard for clay shooting.) Arguments roll on about the relative advantages of the two, but buying any shotgun really centres on two criteria: what do you want the gun for, and how does it fit?

The gauge of the weapon is one of the first choices that determine a shotgun's purpose. The main shotgun gauges, working from smallest to largest, are .410, 28, 16, 20, and 12, with 10-bore, 8-bore and even larger shotguns also available.

Both .410 and 28-bore shotguns are principally suited to shooting small, light game, especially when the shooter wants no recoil, while the 16- and 20-bore guns are good for a wider range of bird shooting, such as pigeon, quail and pheasant, and ground animals like rabbits and hares. The 20-gauge is also an enjoyable

Shot Size

The right shotgun ammunition for hunting is partly a matter of choice. Pellet size – and therefore the number of pellets in each cartridge – varies according to a defined scale. At the most diminutive end of that scale we have no.9 birdshot, of which there would be more than 500 pellets in a typical 28g (1oz) cartridge load. Conversely, each 000 ('triple aught') buckshot has a diameter of 9.1mm (0.36in), and only six would fit into the same load. Naturally, a hunter needs to select the right cartridge for his intended prey type, and this requires experience and solid advice.

Small birds will be handled comfortably by 7–7½ shot, while larger birds (such as ducks) and rabbits require more in the region of 4–6. BB shot to no.2 shot is better suited to high-flying geese or large hares, and 00 buckshot can take on foxes, coyotes and similar larger animals. Remember that the heavier the shot, the further it will fly, therefore giving you a better range over smaller shot.

clay gun for sporting disciplines. An advantage of the small-calibre guns is that they tend to be light, which means they can be comfortably carried around on a day's shoot. Disadvantages can be limited killing power, particularly at range, and expensive shells. This is especially true of more rare gauges such as the 28 and 16.

The 12-gauge shotgun is by far and away the most popular. Depending on the cartridge type selected (an important consideration for any of the gauges), a 12-gauge shotgun will serve the shooter from hunting small ground game up to large wildfowl, and is the definitive clay-shooting gauge. The heavier bores are much more rarely used, and tend to be for those who specialize in long-range wildfowling, where they need to project a great deal of shot up to an unusually high altitude.

Layout and Fit
Once the shooter has decided on a gauge, many other variables come into play. Here are some general guidelines. Barrel length is important. The longer the barrel, the tighter will be the spread of shot at range, hence

long-barrelled 81cm (32in) guns tend to be used more for distance clay disciplines such as trap shooting. A 76cm (30in) gun is a good clay all-rounder and a workable field gun, while the 71cm (28in) barrel serves well for walked-up game and bird shooting, and for clay disciplines like skeet and sporting.

If you want a gun purely for field shooting, stray towards lighter guns of up to 3.4kg (7.5lb) – you have to

Chokes and their Effect

The numbered circles represent the approximate distance in metres at which the spread shot achieves a 102cm (40in) spread using the specific choke.

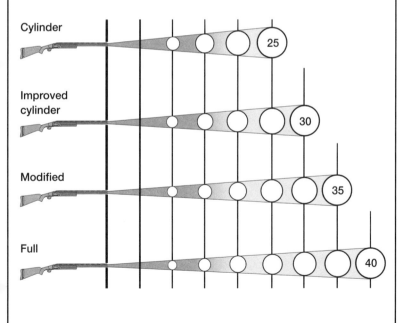

Cylinder — 25

Improved cylinder — 30

Modified — 35

Full — 40

Chokes

In shotgun terminology, the choke refers to the constriction of the barrel at the muzzle, which controls the spread of the shot once it has left the gun. The 'tighter' the choke, the narrower the constriction, and the more the shot pattern is squeezed together over range. Ideally, you want chokes in the gun that put 70 per cent of the shot into a 76cm (30in) circle at your intended range. Chokes are graded according to the following system, and are shown here with the range at which 70 per cent of the shot is within the circle described above:

Extra full – 41m (45yds; 134ft)
Full – 37m (40yds; 121ft)
Modified – 32m (35yds; 105ft)
Improved cylinder – 27m (30yds; 88ft)
Cylinder – 23m (25yds; 75ft)

Chokes are either 'fixed', which means it is integral to the barrel construction, or interchangeable – screw-in chokes that can be changed according to requirements. However, don't become too obsessed with choke changing. In a double gun, a combination of Improved cylinder/Modified or Modified/Full will serve you well in most field hunting situations.

carry one around all day – while for clays, a slightly heavier gun is better. Weightier guns give a more controlled swing, ideal for moving smoothly with a crossing clay, while a lighter gun swings much faster, hence is useful for those snap-shot movements.

Semi-automatic Shotguns

The most obvious difference is that a semi-automatic has a single barrel rather than two barrels. Only one choke pattern, therefore, is in operation, hence the majority (but by

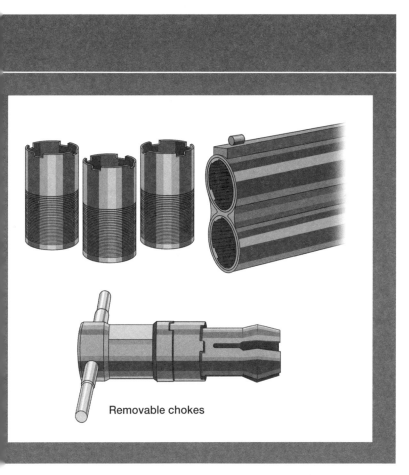

Removable chokes

no means all) of clay shooters prefer the two-choke option of a double-barrelled gun. Furthermore, some clay grounds can be slightly more wary of semi-automatics because they are magazine-fed rather than breech-loaded, hence they cannot be 'seen to be safe' as is the case with a broken-open shotgun. Furthermore, some argue that semi-automatics are much less reliable than break-barrel guns because of their mechanically complex semi-automatic systems. Many of these arguments, on closer

Weatherby SAS

Shotguns aimed at the hunting market often come with a choice of camouflage finishes. Each is tailored to a different terrain type.

inspection, lose their validity. In terms of choke, the semi-automatic shooter with Modified will probably shoot a sporting layout just as well as with a Modified/Improved modified over-and-under. Good safety discipline – particularly muzzle awareness and opening the bolt when not shooting – reassures most fellow shooters. Regarding reliability, I have seen as many misfires and breakdowns with double guns as I have with semi-automatics. However, it is a fact that semi-automatics require much more careful cleaning and handling, because dirt or fouling in a semi-auto mechanism can easily cause a

misfeed. Drop one in the mud and it may well require full stripping.

Semi-automatic Sport

There are many areas where a good semi-automatic is a perfect choice. Depending on the gauge, a semi-automatic's magazine will typically hold three to six cartridges. (Note that the magazine capacity can be limited depending on the country. The UK, for example, limits a semi-automatic's capacity to two shells in the magazine and one in the chamber.) Many bird shooters prefer the greater capacity of a semi-automatic over a double gun,

particularly for sports such as pigeon shooting or wildfowling, in which multiple shots often have to be taken in quick succession before an entire flock gets out of range.

Semi-automatics also have particularly light recoil – the gas, inertia or recoil mechanism soaks up much of the kick. Not only does this mean that semi-automatics are good for small-framed people or those suffering with shoulder complaints, but also that these guns are ideal for taking very heavy hunting loads, such as those found in 89mm (3.5in) shells. (This is another good reason why wildfowlers often prefer the

semi-automatic, the big magnum cartridges being used against large or high-flying geese.)

The greater percentage of semi-automatic shotguns are operated using gas. In this system, some of the gas created by the propellant powder when burnt is siphoned downwards through a port in the barrel into a cylinder set beneath the barrel. The gas drives a piston backwards, and this rearward force, through a series of connected mechanisms, unlocks the bolt and forces it backwards.

During this stage of movement the spent cartridge is extracted and

Using a Pump Gun

Working the action of a pump-actions shotgun causes the weapon to move off the aim point, but an experienced user can quickly re-acquire his target if necessary.

ejected. Finally, the recoil spring forces the bolt to return forward, picking up a new cartridge and driving it forward into the chamber for the next shot.

The other methods of semi-automatic operation are recoil and inertia. In both methods the gun uses the force of recoil alone to operate the weapon, the recoil action using

the force of the barrel and bolt assembly being driven backwards, the latter using the energy stored in an inertia spring as the moveable parts of the gun go backwards. All are sound operating systems if maintained, with recoil and inertia having the advantage that no gases are vented into a piston system, but are all kept within the barrel.

Semi-Automatic Fire

The first time I fired a semi-automatic shotgun was an interesting experience. It was easy enough to handle firing single shots, but under rapid fire I found that I needed to treat it with more respect or it would climb off my shoulder and hit me in the cheekbone with its stock. Once I learned to lock it in properly, it was no problem, but I learned my lesson – don't be casual with an unfamiliar weapon, and don't assume that you can control it easily until you've tried.

Pump Guns

Pump-action shotguns are single-barrel weapons, in which cartridges are contained in an under-barrel tubular magazine. The cartridges are loaded into the weapon, and ejected when fired, by the manual action of cocking a slide around the magazine. One immediate advantage of the pump-action over the double-gun is ammunition capacity; some pump guns can have six or seven cartridges in the magazine, meaning that a hunter can open up with multiple shots at flocks of geese or other crowded targets. The other crowning benefit of the pump gun is its awesome reliability. The manual mechanism is very forgiving in grubby conditions, and will keep operating even when the action is moderately contaminated with dirt, dust or even snow. Such reliability makes pump guns very dependable hunting weapons. Their simplicity

also means that they tend to be available on meagre budgets.

Semi-auto shotguns are rather like pump-action guns, but with the reloading process performed automatically by recoil or gas operation rather than manually. The performance characteristics of the shot is no different from a pump gun, but the reloading can be extremely quick, making the process of taking multiple shots at targets of opportunity that much faster. Recoil is also softened in a semi-auto. The trade-off is that semi-auto guns have more complicated mechanisms, making them more prone to jamming than their manually operated cousins.

Whichever shotgun you choose is down to preference, purpose and budget. Before we turn to rifles, however, there are some general rules to bear in mind when handling a shotgun:

Misfires and Hangfires

With modern ammunition, a 'hangfire' (where the round does not immediately fire, but goes off after a short delay) is a rare event, and in most cases the delay is much less than a second. All the same, a weapon that has misfired should be aimed at the target or a suitable backstop for a suitable period. Many ranges specify 30 seconds to be absolutely sure the round is a dud, although some less formal gun enthusiasts suggest that 'long enough to give it a good cussing' is sufficient. A wait of at least several seconds is required, just in case.

- Keep both eyes open when shooting, staring hard at your target and utilizing the advantage of stereoscopic vision.
- Place almost all your body weight on the front foot and lean forward into the shotgun. The only exception is when taking high overhead shots (passing from front to back), in which you might find it more comfortable to drop the body weight on to the back foot as the gun follows the target.
- Practice constantly to get used to lead 'pictures' – the visual gap between the muzzles and the target at the point of firing.
- Keep the gun moving as you take the shot – aim to spread the shot across the target. If you stop as you squeeze the trigger, you are likely to miss behind the target.

Ammunition

Ammunition is another area where a little knowledge goes a long way. Some ammunition types are sub-optimal for certain applications, and may be illegal. It may be necessary to modify or at least optimize a weapon for certain ammunition types, and of course it is often possible to keep costs down by using less expensive but equally effective ammunition or selecting the optimal choice of load and thus needing to shoot less often. In a few cases, the right ammunition can be a lifesaver, such as when hunting dangerous game, and can ensure a quick and humane kill that does not require a wounded animal to be tracked for a lengthy period.

Calibre. Rifle and handgun calibres are normally measured either in inches or millimetres. There are no sporting guns with a calibre of greater

Pump Gun Action

Most pump-action weapons use a tubular magazine under the barrel, but other configurations are available. The principle is the same in each case: the first movement opens the breech and ejects the round; the second chambers the next and closes the breech ready to fire.

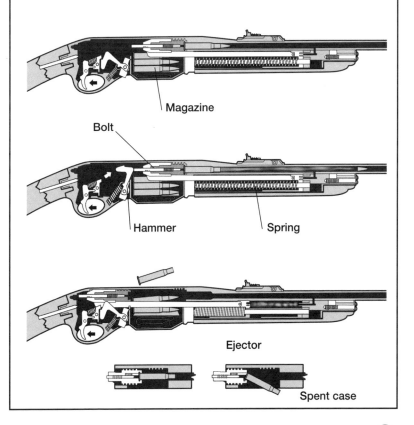

Magazine

Bolt

Hammer

Spring

Ejector

Spent case

than an inch, so a decimal is used. This describes the diameter of the weapon's bore; a larger bore allows a bigger and heavier bullet, i.e. a more powerful weapon. Calibres in inches do not indicate the length of the cartridge, but this is implicit as standardized sizes have been in use for generations.

It is not always obvious whether a given calibre refers to handgun or rifle ammunition but, again, certain calibres are associated with particular weapons. Thus .45 ACP is a well-known (and powerful) handgun calibre; .270 Winchester is a popular rifle calibre. Rifle ammunition tends to be smaller in diameter but will have a much longer case than handgun rounds, resulting in a higher muzzle velocity. This is obvious when calibres are given in millimetres, since the

Types of Round

Rifle and handgun ammunition almost always uses a full metal cartridge case, but most shotgun ammunition has a soft plastic or paper hull.

9mm   .44 Magnum   7.62mm   5.56mm

format is (diameter) x (length). For example, 9x19mm is a common handgun cartridge; the much longer 5.56x45mm is obviously for a rifle.

Weight. The mass of a projectile does not depend entirely upon its size. In any given calibre, bullet weights can vary. Weights are normally given in grams or grains; the latter a rather archaic measure equal to 1/7000 of a pound. A heavier bullet will generally penetrate a target better but will have a lower muzzle velocity for the same amount of propellant.

Pellets. Shotguns use a smooth barrel, since rifling affects the pattern of shot coming out of the weapon. A group of small pellets does not seal as well into the barrel as a single bullet, which reduces muzzle velocity. Pellets lose energy quickly as they are not aerodynamic, but on the plus side a pattern of shot is more likely to achieve a hit than a single bullet and multiple impacts are often better at bringing down a target. Shot does not overpenetrate (go right through the target and out the other side) like a bullet might, which can have implications for safety.

12 gauge shell

Magnum Ammunition

The term Magnum simply means 'big' and was coined to describe a pistol cartridge that was a little longer than standard and held more propellant. This increased muzzle velocity and therefore the power of the weapon.

Birdshot

Birdshot shells contain a large number of small pellets, increasing the chances of a hit by putting a pattern of shot where, with luck, the bird will be. Heavier shot is not necessary for small game such as birds.

Birdshot and buckshot. A greater variety of ammunition is available for shotguns than for rifles. Common loads are birdshot and buckshot. Birdshot is, as the name suggests, primarily intended for bringing down small game such as birds. It consists of many small pellets that create a relatively dense cloud, greatly increasing the chances of a hit. Birdshot is not heavy enough to kill larger animals, so a smaller number of larger projectiles are used. This is termed 'buckshot'; the name implies that it is useful against larger and more robust game, such as deer. Solid ammunition is also available for use in shotguns. A single projectile will travel further and allow more accurate shooting as well as increasing knockdown power for dangerous game. Solid ammunition

can be used to hunt with a shotgun in places where rifles are not permitted. However, it is prohibited or controlled under the laws of some countries.

Unusual ammo. Various exotic ammunition is also available, but most of it is for law-enforcement or home defence applications. Some specialist shells might be more effective than standard buckshot against tough game like hog. The manufacturers tend to claim their products are superior – but they would, wouldn't they? Opinions are divided about these shells, whereas birdshot, buckshot and solid slug are well-proven and known to work well in their intended role.

Ammunition Safety

Whatever the weapon, using the

Mossberg 500

Pump-action guns usually provide great durability, but with modern slide systems they are a little slower on the reload than many semi-automatic shotguns. The Mossberg 500 shotguns are a popular entry-level range. The Model 500 may be easily affordable, but Mossberg emphasizes that the gun has passed U.S. Army military specification tests, probably the world's toughest proving examination of any weapon. Model 500 shotguns cross many different formats. The basic Model 500 is available in 12, 20 and .410 gauges, and all models come with 76mm (3in) chambers as standard.

Barrel lengths run from a compact 47cm (18.5in) through to 71cm (28in). Most of the Model 500 barrels are ported, helping to reduce recoil and muzzle flip and thereby facilitating more accurate rapid

fire. A standard Model 500 holds five 70mm (2.75in) shells in its magazine and one in the chamber, the magazine capacity being reduced by one for 76mm (3in) shells. All versions of the Model 500 come with features such as ambidextrous safety switches and either fixed chokes or Accu-Choke multichokes (suitable for steel shot).

Specifications: Mossberg 500 All-Purpose Field
Gauge/calibre: 12, 20, .410
Barrel length: 61cm (24in), 66cm (26in), 71cm (28in)
Weight: 3.4kg (7.5lb)
Mechanism: pump action
Chokes: fixed or Accu-Choke multichokes

Rifle Bullets

Each type of bullet performs differently. As a very general rule, softer and rounder bullets expand much more in the wound, causing greater damage and an increased chance of a quick kill. Other designs are intended to improve velocity or accuracy, sometimes at the expense of wounding capability.

Round nose

Hollow point

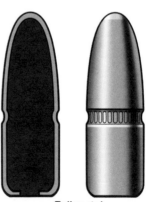

Full metal jacket

Partition
bullet

Boat tail

Spire point

correct ammunition is important to safety. Most mass-produced ammunition is well within the safety tolerances for the weapon it is made for, but some specialist rounds require a more robust gun. Using overpowered ammunition can result in anything from excessive recoil, which is not a particularly serious hazard but can make it hard to hit anything, to a burst firing chamber. Hand-loaded ammunition can vary somewhat in quality and performance, depending on how skilled and careful the producer was. Reloads are cheaper than new ammunition, and are normally fine unless badly made but can vary quite significantly in performance, which impairs accuracy.

Some hand-loaders like to produce their own specialist ammunition. Mostly this is fine, but an overenthusiastic 'hot load' can damage a weapon or worse. It is wise therefore only to use hand-loaded ammunition from people you know and trust, or to learn to do it yourself to an acceptable standard of both quality and consistency.

Old ammunition, batches bought cheaply from importers or which have been sold off as surplus can be a cheap way to obtain a decent quantity for target practice or fun shooting, but ammunition can

Hunting rifles designed for shooting game tend to use high-powered ammunition.

Exotic Shotgun Ammunition

Some 'exotic' shotgun shells are actually pretty utilitarian, although there is much debate about their usefulness. Compound shells containing both heavy and light shot, or certain kinds of super-heavy buckshot, might be useful under some circumstances. Other exotic rounds are aimed at a different market segment; rock salt or steel tacks for use against intruders, frangible door breaching rounds and heavy steel flechettes (which are illegal in many places), and similar specialist rounds, are not really of that much interest to sport shooters. Specialist shells for use against a zombie attack have recently been introduced onto the market. Really.

degrade or might not have been manufactured to a particularly good standard. You certainly cannot rely on old ammunition to perform consistently, and problems are far more likely. Unless you are sufficiently experienced to avoid pitfalls, it is usually best to pass up what seems like a bargain – an accident, damage to your gun or a lengthy session digging out a thoroughly jammed round can make an apparent bargain rather more expensive.

Ammunition can create a hazard in two ways – when it goes off as it is supposed to, and when it does not. A round that is fired produces a great deal of hot gas that comes out of the barrel. Even a blank round does this; you should never point any weapon at anything you do not intend to shoot, and firing a blank at a person can still inflict serious injuries. In addition, the cartridge and the gun itself will become hot.

Picking up a hot cartridge can burn the fingers, and weapons that eject the spent case can sometimes throw it somewhere painful. Being hit in the face or body by a hot case can cause a flinch, which is dangerous when holding a live weapon. The only answer is to learn not to wave the weapon about when a hot cartridge case hits you in the nose.

Environmental issues are related to safety concerns, but mainly deal with the impact of shooting on the environment. Some kinds of ammunition contain harmful chemicals, notably lead, which can harm wildlife.

Sights

The sights you use on your rifle are obviously central to the efficiency of your hunting. There are basically two types of sight you will use: open sights and telescopic sights. Open sights are the non-magnifying sights that generally come fitted to the rifle as standard. The classic arrangement is a V-shaped adjustable rear sight that corresponds with a post-type front sight, but there are variations, such as aperture sights. In general, open sights are generally used for hunting either small creatures at very close ranges or fast-moving, large and dangerous prey, when the hunter might need to fire multiple follow-up shots without taking his eyes off the target. In most other circumstances, a telescopic sight is required for the optimum accuracy.

When buying a telescopic sight, expert advice at point of sale is essential. Scopes come in a bewildering range of formats and magnifications, and a poor choice can result in missed kills or wounded animals. A basic consideration is the magnification and diameter of the objective lens, expressed in a formula such as 6x40 – meaning a magnification power of six and an objective lens diameter of 40mm (1.5in). The larger the objective lens figure, the better the scope will be for use in low-light conditions (the larger the lens, the more light it lets in).

Adjusting Telescopic Sights

A telescopic sight, no matter how expensive, will be little more than useless if it is not zeroed properly. Learning how to zero a telescopic sight to the point of impact of the rifle is best done on a shooting range under expert tuition. You will also need to understand the relationship between the gradations on the reticle (the cross hairs that form the aiming point in your sight) and different ranges of shot – again your shooting coach should provide you with advice. Finally, ensure that you have high-quality mounts securing your sight to the rifle, and re-zero the gun if either the sights or the mounts receive a hard knock. Remember that your chief goal as a hunter is a clean kill – you owe that at least to the animal that is about to feed you.

Telescopic Sights

Telescopic sights work by using two lenses: one to magnify and one to focus the image. The sight must be adjusted to account for distance – light travels in straight lines but bullets don't.

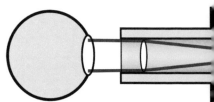

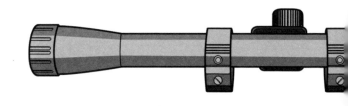

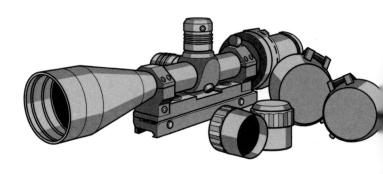

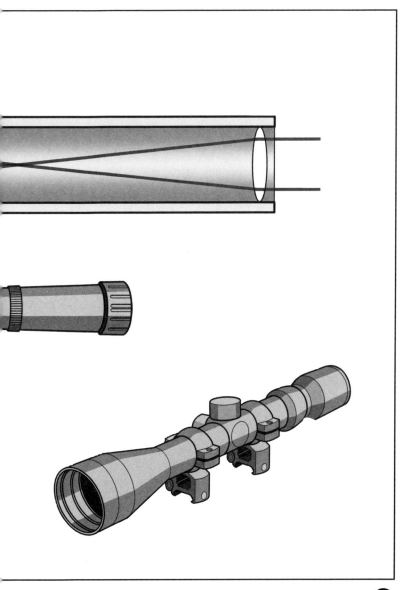

High-magnification lens might seem desirable, but note that the greater the power, the less the field of view, making it more difficult to acquire targets.

Many modern telescopic sights now feature adjustable magnification. These systems are undoubtedly useful, as they allow the sight to be adapted for the specific hunting conditions. However, ensure that you don't spend your time constantly adjusting the power – the sight is only part of the accurate shot, and won't do all the work for you.

Guns and the Law

A working knowledge of relevant laws surrounding weapons, ammunition and hunting is essential if you want to stay out of court. Local laws can sometimes be quite complex, so it is always worth checking up on any variations that might exist if you hunt or shoot in a new area; assumptions can be dangerous. Transporting guns across a state line in the USA can be problematical enough; taking them from one country to another is likely to be more trouble than it is worth. Unless you are an Olympic-standard shooter or want to impress foreign royalty with your prestigious firearms, it is usually simpler to make arrangements to hire guns than to battle through all the paperwork required to take your own with you.

In general, there are three main areas of interest: obtaining and owning a firearm, possessing a firearm in a given place, and specific hunting laws.

In many areas it is necessary to have a permit in order to legally own a gun or ammunition. In general, shotguns are subject to the least regulation, followed by rifles, then handguns, but this varies from place to place. Certain types of ammunition and specific weapons may be subject to additional regulation, and some may be prohibited.

Military-type weapons such as automatic rifles and submachineguns, as well as very large calibre rifles, tend to be outlawed for private use, or at least very strictly controlled. This does not generally affect sports shooters, but 'assault weapons' are subject to changing legislation and this can impact upon sports shooters at times. For example, certain types of semi-automatic shotgun have a pistol grip and a detachable magazine, taking them close to the definition of an assault weapon.

Assuming your guns are legal in the first place, you need to be aware of laws governing transporting them and carrying them in a public place. Some areas require transportation in a locked container; others do not. In many regions it is legal to have a loaded firearm, concealed or openly carried, in areas where hunting is likely to take place, but there may be restrictions in place and it is wise to find out ahead of time what they are.

Sight Recticles

Telescopic sights improve accurate shooting at longer ranges... providing the shooter knows how to use one. In theory, placing the crosshairs or aim point on the target should ensure a hit, but only if the sight is properly adjusted and the range has been accurately estimated.

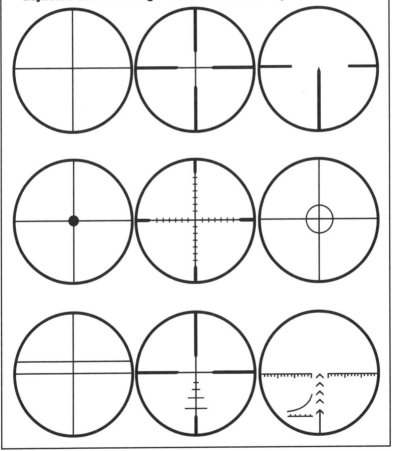

Practical Shooting

Practical pistol and practical shotgun events simulate real combat conditions, providing a different kind of test to target shooting. Practical events require different guns to hunting, and usually attract a different segment of the shooting community.

Even if your guns are legal and it is permitted to have them in the area where you are shooting, that does not automatically mean that you can just shoot what you like. Some game is subject to restrictions on when or where it can be shot, or the numbers that can be taken. Some weapons can only be used against certain targets. One notable restriction is that in many areas rifles cannot be used for hunting, but it may be legal to use a shotgun with a rifled barrel to shoot slugs at deer or turkey.

If you are in an area where hunting is common, and are dressed for hunting and carrying the right guns for hunting, then law enforcement personnel will (quite reasonably) assume that you are there to hunt. Excuses like claiming that you actually intend just a little target practice or have the guns in case of animal attack during your camping trip will not get you out of a court appearance. Neither will ignorance of the law.

So, if you are going out hunting, you need to know beforehand what permits are required. You need to ensure that your firearms and ammunition are legal in the area you are hunting, and for use against the game you will meet. Environmental laws, such as prohibitions on lead shot, are every bit as serious as other restrictions. Knowing what you can and cannot do will prevent a hunting trip from becoming an expensive day at the courthouse.

The basic principles of shooting are much the same, no matter what the weapon or the target may be. The overriding rule is that if you are not sure a shot is safe to take, then don't take it. Assuming that it is safe to shoot, then certain principles apply to all weapons.

A Stable Platform

The key to accurate shooting is to create a stable platform to fire from, using your body to support the weapon, and to always maintain the same relationship between eye, sights and muzzle. This is easier said than done, of course.

The weapon must be held firmly and kept steady. If a moving target is being tracked, or the gun has to move for any other reason, then movements need to be smooth. This does not necessarily mean that the gun has to move slowly, but it must not be jerked around. It is possible to shoot very well with a pistol held in one hand, but normally both hands are used to support the weapon. If the gun has a shoulder stock, then this should be pulled in tight to the shoulder and not allowed to move around at all. Movement may spoil

....

The sound of a shot will usually startle the quarry, causing it to flee and become a very difficult target. A second shot will often be impossible.

3

There are two key principles to shooting well: learning to put all your shots into as small an area as possible, and learning to put that area exactly where you want it. If you cannot do both, you will not reliably hit your target.

Basic Principles of Shooting

Aim Supports

Supporting the rifle on something is less tiring than holding it ready for a long period. A sand sock can be used as a passive support, between the rifle and an uneven surface such as a rock, or can be actively used to alter the aim point by squeezing it slightly.

Sand sock

your aim, and it can also cause the weapon to hurt the shoulder or smack you in the cheekbone.

The stock also needs to be selected or adjusted for the individual user. A badly fitting stock results in an awkward firing position, and can transfer recoil energy to the user in a most unpleasant manner.

A good shooting position and properly fitting stock create a precise relationship between the shooter's eye and the weapon's sights. If this relationship is always the same, then

shooting – which is not the same as accurate shooting. Precision is all about the size of 'group' you create with a series of shots at a given range. If you can consistently put your shots in a small group, then you are shooting precisely, but of course if the group is well off target, then you are not shooting accurately.

Contact with the ground or whatever else you may be standing on is important. As a rule, the more contact you have with the ground, the more stable your position will be. This lying position offers more support than kneeling, which in turn offers more support than standing. This of course assumes that the ground is stable. Lying on loose rocks that slide about every time you move, or standing on a less-than-secure platform halfway up a tree, will seriously impair accuracy even if it is not unsafe or uncomfortable. You can also lean, sit or rest your weapon against objects, but again something stable should be chosen. Objects that can move about are not a good place to rest your weapon.

It is possible to hold a weapon quite awkwardly and still shoot well, but this is the exception rather than the rule. A good firing position aligns the weapon naturally with your body, and eliminates tension and strain from your body while you aim. A gun that is too heavy for you will require too much effort to hold up, and this is not only tiring; if you are straining to

one variable that can affect accuracy is eliminated.

Thus holding the weapon is a matter of creating a known relationship between eye and sights, and not allowing the weapon to wander around. This has the effect of allowing precise

Learn to Shoot Safely Before You Learn to Shoot Well

Firearms are tools, just like any other, and like all tools they need to be handled with care. A mishandled hammer will smash your thumb; a slip with a kitchen knife will make you bleed. It rarely happens though, because we recognize the danger and take adequate precautions. The same applies to firearms. With proper handling, a gun should only ever pose a hazard to what it is being fired at. Indeed, that is the underlying purpose of firearms training. Long before you begin learning to hit a target, you should have learned how only to endanger what you are firing at.

hold the weapon on target, then it will not stay on target. A gun that is light enough to handle is essential to good shooting unless you intend to fire from a rest.

Precision and Accuracy

Once you have learned to shoot precisely, you can then train yourself to put your small group where you want it. This is a matter of practice, observing where your shots go and adjusting your aim point until you can put a small group of shots into the place you want them. In reality, accuracy and precision tend to be developed at the same time, but accuracy is of little use without precision. You may be able to accurately put your aim point right on target, but if your group is huge, then

you may still miss by a large margin. Conversely, there is no point in putting all your shots into a tiny group that is vastly off target.

In order to facilitate accuracy and precision, you need to eliminate factors that might disrupt your aim, such as movement of the weapon as you fire. Even your breathing can take a long-range shot off target, so shooters often use a technique of letting out half a breath, then taking final aim and shooting before letting the rest out. Holding your breath for too long will disrupt your aim, however, so there is a 'window' of just a few seconds to aim and shoot before you need to start over. Breath control is not so necessary when shooting at shorter distances, but there are other factors that need to be eliminated.

Improving Your Shooting

If shots are consistently off target in the same direction, then it is highly likely that you are making a specific error. The correction chart indicates the most likely problem based on shot location relative to the target.

Pistol Correction Chart
(Right Hand)

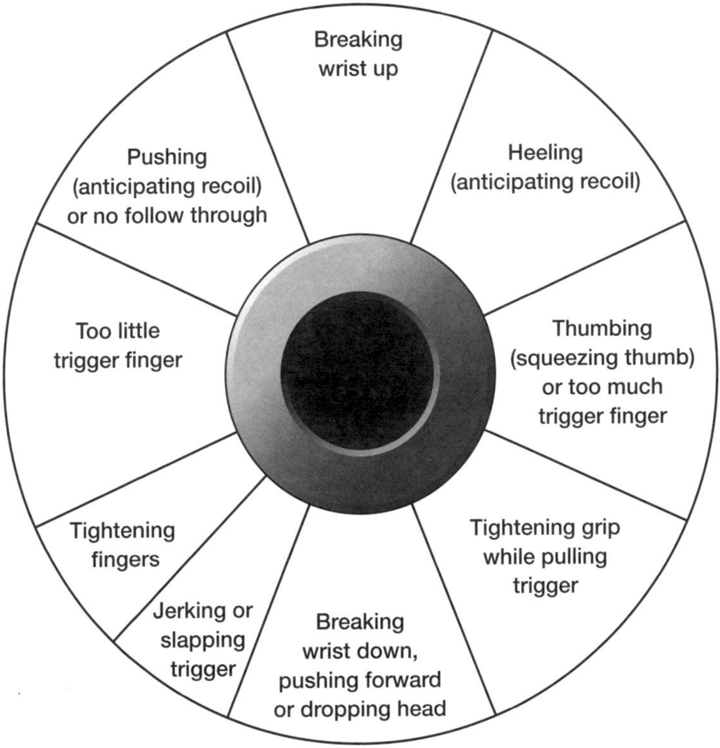

Breaking
wrist up

Pushing
(anticipating recoil)
or no follow through

Heeling
(anticipating recoil)

Too little
trigger finger

Thumbing
(squeezing thumb)
or too much
trigger finger

Tightening
fingers

Tightening grip
while pulling
trigger

Jerking or
slapping
trigger

Breaking
wrist down,
pushing forward
or dropping head

Accuracy can be impaired by anticipating your shot. If you shoot a powerful weapon with heavy recoil, then you may tend to flinch just at the moment the weapon discharges. This can pull the shot off target, as can trying to control expected recoil just before it happens. In this case there is a tendency to push the barrel down just as you expect the weapon to discharge, rather than controlling recoil after the shot is on its way. Curing a tendency to flinch can be a lengthy process.

Some shooters just give up and adjust their sights to hit high, artificially compensating for their tendency to flinch. This can work but it is not good shooting.

One way to cure a tendency to flinch is to practice by dry-firing – going through the motions of shooting without ammunition loaded. Hold the weapon on target and gradually increase trigger pressure until it 'fires', then hold it on target for a couple of seconds with the trigger pulled all the way.

Holding a Handgun

Opinions vary about the perfect two-handed grip, but overall what is most important is that the weapon is firmly held and that the grip is the same each time. If each shot is fired from a slightly different hand position, accuracy will suffer enormously.

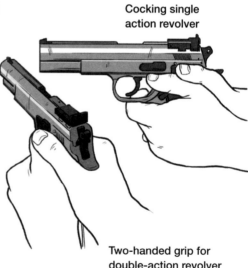

Cocking single action revolver

Two-handed grip for double-action revolver

Trigger Pressure

You should not try to anticipate the moment of firing, but increase trigger pressure until the weapon responds. This is often termed a 'surprise break' as the trigger break should come as a surprise. Once you can reliably dry-fire in this manner without flinching, apply the same technique with a loaded weapon. If you find yourself flinching, go back to dry-firing.

Ideally, the firearm is held on target, or tracks the target, while trigger pressure is gradually increased. The shooter does not try to anticipate the perfect moment for a shot, as this leads to a tendency to snatch or yank the trigger. Instead, the shot is set up, accepting that the sights may 'wobble' a little during this period (the dispersion this causes is surprisingly small) and the trigger gradually squeezed until the weapon discharges. So long as this occurs within the period that the shot is set up properly, the target will be hit.

A well-adjusted trigger is important to accuracy. If your trigger

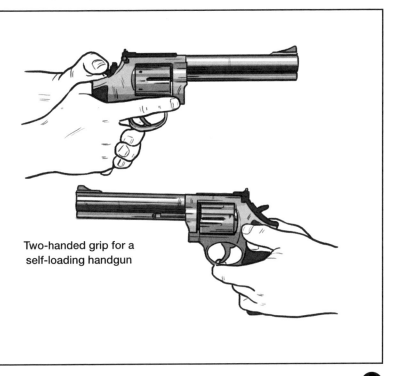

Two-handed grip for a
self-loading handgun

Krieghoff KX-5

The KX-5 builds upon the KS-5 Special Trap gun, adding more technological refinements. With a 76cm (30in) or 81cm (32in) barrel (trap shooters prefer longer barrel lengths to improve reach and shot-pattern density at range), the KX-5 also has a fully adjustable rib. Straight from the factory the rib is set to produce a 65 per cent/35 per cent pattern (meaning 65 per cent of the pattern is thrown above the point of aim). However, a dial control at the muzzle allows the shooter to make dramatic alterations to this pattern, up to 90 per cent high or down to a flat 50 per cent/50 per cent.

The barrel has a high, tapered rib with spacious ventilation to prevent heat distortion from the barrel spoiling the shooter's visual acquisition of the target.

Krieghoff Trap guns come fitted with a Monte Carlo stock (that is, a raised cheek-piece section) with an adjustable comb for a precise custom fit. To further personalize the weapon for the user, the trigger

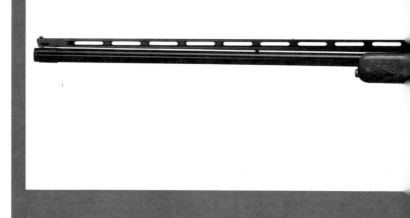

is adjustable for length of pull. The fore-end has a push-button lock to attach it to the barrels; this, according to Krieghoff, 'providing a better and stronger latch to the barrel'.

Although it is a single-barrel gun, the KX-5 comes with multichokes in three constrictions – Modified, Improved Modified and Full – although the gun can take any of Krieghoff's full range of chokes, which run from Cylinder to Super Full.

Specifications: Krieghoff KX-5
Gauge/calibre: 12
Barrel length: 76cm (30in), 81cm (32in)
Weight: 3.9kg (8.75lb)
Ejector type: automatic ejectors
Chokes: multichokes

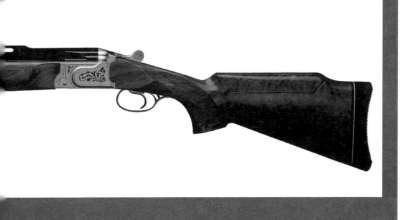

pull is too light then your weapon may go off before you are ready for it, which is dangerous as well as inaccurate. Too heavy and the effort of working the trigger will cause the weapon to move off the aim point. A crisp break, combined with a pull that is light enough to be easy but heavy enough that you know you are doing it, will allow you to shoot to the best of your ability. However, it is wise to understand that equipment is only an enabler – a bad gun can spoil good technique, but an excellent one will not improve bad shooting.

Aim

Aiming is more than just pointing the gun in the right direction. For an accurate shot, especially over long distances, you must maintain the natural alignment of the weapon and your whole body, turning the whole structure if necessary rather than trying to stay still and track the target with just the muzzle of the weapon. The techniques for this vary somewhat from one weapon to another, and are also affected by the environment in which the weapon is to be used.

For a static target, aiming is simply a matter of pointing the weapon at where the target is and shooting, but matters become more complicated when trying to hit something that is on the move. There are two basic techniques, both of which have the same intent, which is to ensure that

the target and the projectile arrive at the same point at the same moment. A bullet or shot pattern travels much faster than a running deer or a flying bird, but all the same the target may move a significant distance in the time between the decision to shoot and the arrival of the projectile.

It is not always possible to predict where a target might veer or swerve, or when a stationary animal might take off running. However, an experienced hunter can tell where a target will not go – a bird on the wing can only turn so much and a running animal will tend to go around rather than through obstructions, even fairly loose ones such as clumps of grass. With this information, it is possible to pick an aim point that the target is likely to pass through. By shooting at the right moment, the projectile is timed to arrive at the same time as the target. This technique is sometimes useful where game is likely to run down a predictable trail, but is less effective against birds, as there are fewer features in the sky against which to judge speed.

An alternative, and more generally effective, technique is to track the target, swinging the gun smoothly so that the muzzle moves a little faster than the target is moving. When it gets far enough ahead to compensate for the flight time of the projectile, the shooter takes his shot. Leading the target in this manner works best when the target is moving predictably; a

Aim Point

The diagram below indicates the sight picture and impact point for telescopic and blade sights.

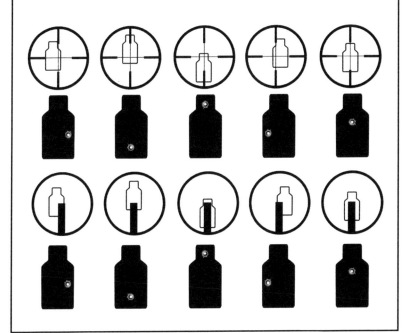

wildly veering bird is hard to lead in this manner.

The process is made more difficult still by wind conditions, although shooting directly into or with the wind helps eliminate this problem. Similarly, a target that is coming directly at the shooter is easier to hit, such as birds being driven towards a gun line. A gun with a fast 'lock time' is also some help; the shorter the delay between pulling the trigger and the weapon firing, the less time the target has to move or change direction.

Ballistic Arc

Bullets do not travel in a straight line. They are pulled down by gravity, which creates a ballistic arc, and slowed by air friction. Beyond very short ranges it is necessary to fire upwards in order to arc the shot to the target – firing straight forward will result in the projectile hitting the ground long before it reaches its intended destination.

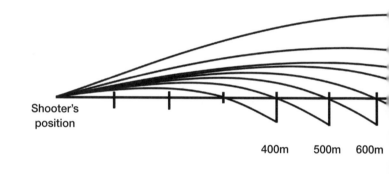

Shooter's position

400m   500m   600m

Nothing can be done about the flight time of shot or bullet, other than to use higher-velocity ammunition, but any reduction in the delay between the decision to shoot and the arrival of the shot increases the chance of a hit.

Long-range Shooting

When firing at extremely long distances, the slightest movement of the weapon can cause the shot to miss by a large margin. One solution is to shoot from a rest, which can be improvised in the field or custom-produced. Rests range from a handy rock or a nearby fence, through custom-made and improvised bipods, to a shooting bench at the range. When firing from a rest, many shooters like to use a 'sand sock', which is a bag (or an actual sock if you prefer) filled with sand or plastic beads.

Rather than supporting the weapon with the hand, it rests on the sock, which is in the hand. Squeezing the sock will raise the barrel a little, giving very precise control

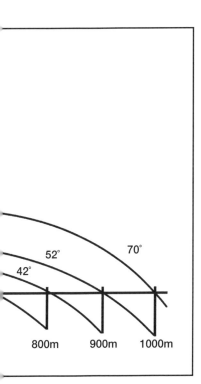

52°

70°

42°

800m   900m   1000m

Pistol Shooting Mechanics

Handguns are intrinsically less accurate than rifles for several reasons. Their shorter barrel results in a lower muzzle velocity and therefore a less flat trajectory, and there is no shoulder stock to support the weapon. Even when both hands are used to support the firearm, the short gap between the hands means that recoil is harder to control and small movements of the weapon produce a greater deviation in aim point.

Pistols are normally used for target shooting and competitions that simulate combat conditions, but they are used by some hunters. In 'practical' or 'combat' shooting competitions, the shooter will often run a course and fire from several points or on the move. This requires high-speed 'point and shoot' skills and a stance that is typical of self-defence or combat shooting. Usually the weapon is fired from a solid two-handed stance, although some shooters will use a one-handed stance when appropriate.

over elevation without affecting the aim point laterally. A similar effect is obtained by holding the weapon by the front sling swivel (if it has one), with the sling passing through the fist and the hand resting on a support, e.g. the ground. Tightening the fist will alter elevation. This technique is not effective for a weapon that has to be swung to follow a target, so is normally used for target shooting or 'trapping' a target by aiming at a known point and waiting for the target to approach it.

Stance

The pistol-shooting stance most commonly used for recreational and practical pistol competition is some variation on the 'weaver' or 'isosceles' stance. The dominant hand (the one that fires your pistol, usually the right) is back, with the supporting-side pushed forward and the body at roughly 45 degrees to the target.

Gripping a Handgun

There is much debate on exactly how to grip a handgun for accurate shooting. At the very least, the weapon must be firmly gripped in the hand and unable to wander around under recoil.

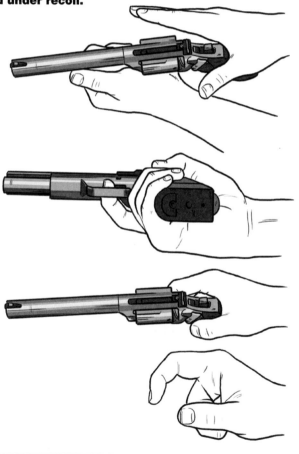

Two-handed Standing Position

The isosceles shooting stance creates a triangle, with the weapon at its apex and the shooter's shoulders as the base. It is strong and stable, making it a good place to start learning to shoot well.

This position is not unlike a boxer's fighting stance. The weapon is firmly held in both hands and pushed towards the target, with the supporting hand pulling the weapon back towards the shooter to create a good front-and-back lock.

Shooting well in this manner is a matter of learning how to line up the body with the weapon as an extension of it, and to a great extent judge by eye where the muzzle is pointing. Bullet drop and wind effects tend to be minimal at close range, so it is possible simply to look at the target and shoot it, providing your stance is good enough to create that all-important constant relationship between eye and weapon. Many shooters advocate using binocular vision (both eyes open) but closing one eye is an equally valid technique – if it works well for you, then do it.

The advantage of the 'combat' stance is that is can be quickly adopted after moving, and it offers the best weapon stability possible with a handgun other than on a rest. A two-handed stance also helps control recoil, which is highly important when hunting with a very powerful handgun. This stance is used in many target-shooting competitions, but for Olympic-style target shooting a one-handed stance is specified.

In a one-handed pistol-shooting stance, the dominant side is forward, with the body sideways on to the target and the arm outstretched. Aiming is down a straight arm, which requires a light gun to avoid excessive effort being necessary to keep the weapon on target. The other hand needs to be kept out of the way and still; any movement of the rear arm will twist the body and pull the weapon off target. Some shooters just stick their hand in a pocket; others have a favoured position.

One variant on this position is a traditional pistol duelling stance, with the unarmed hand behind the back and the body very upright. This stance combined ease of aiming with minimized target area, which was important in a 'competition' where the opponent was shooting back. It was also used for military marksmanship up to the early 20th century, although it is rather too formal for normal combat conditions. It is not difficult to shoot even a fairly heavy gun from this position; the author has fired an original .455 Webley MkVI revolver from this position and despite being heavy in every regard – weapon, trigger pull and recoil – the experience was highly pleasant and good accuracy was possible.

Rifle Shooting Mechanics

Rifles offer the shooter the greatest range of firing positions. They all have certain concepts in common – natural alignment of the weapon and body, weapon pulled in good and tight to

One-handed Standing Position

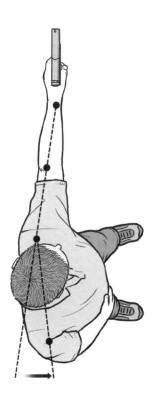

When shooting one-handed, the key is to create a natural alignment of the body with the target, eliminating as much tension as possible to avoid the weapon being pulled off target.

Standing Position

In the basic standing position, the stock is pulled in firmly to the shoulder and the cheek rests on it, creating a constant relationship between eyes and sights.
The aim is to create a solid structure with the upper body and weapon.

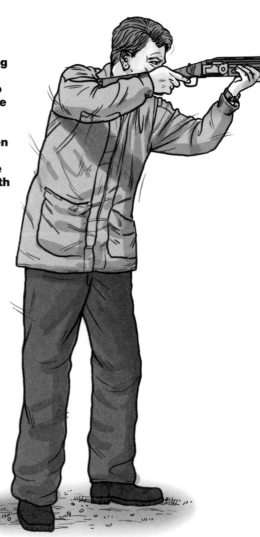

the shoulder, constant relationship between eye and sights, and maximum stability – but each is adapted for a different set of circumstances.

Standing Firing Position

A standing firing position is suitable for almost any situation, and may be the only realistic option – most shooters prefer not to kneel or lie down in a swamp if they can avoid it. A standing firing position is in many ways similar to the 'combat' pistol stance; supporting side forward, body angled at about 45 degrees. Weight on the balls of your feet, with the left foot pointing at the target. The rifle is pulled in firmly to the shoulder, with the dominant arm more or less horizontal with the elbow pointing out at 90 degrees and the supporting elbow pointing down.

This basic position has been taught by national militaries for generations and has proven very effective in quick and accurate shooting at both static and moving targets. If the target is moving, it is tracked by twisting at the hips, pivoting the whole structure constructed from head, arms, torso and rifle rather than trying to angle the weapon. If the target goes outside your comfortable arc of fire, reposition or seek a different target.

Individuals have their own variants on this basic position; what

Browning BL-22

The Browning BL-22 evokes the traditions of the West with its Henry-like appearance and its classic lever action. It is ideal for those wanting a light and tough field gun, especially young shooters. The basic BL-22 is the Grade I, which gives a good feel for the rest of the series (at the time of writing there are seven BL-22 models in total). It is a .22 rimfire weapon, chambered for .22 S, L and LR. Barrel length is a short 51cm (20in) and the overall finish is very plain and clean, with a blued receiver. Adjustable open sights are fitted – there is a bead front post and a folding-leaf rear sight – but the receiver is also grooved for scope mounts. With the open sights, shots of up to and over 50m (164ft) can be taken, while fitting a scope allows the shooter to utilize the full range of the .22 rounds.

The BL-22 guns use lever action to cycle rounds in from the under-barrel tubular magazine. The total capacity of the magazine is 15 rounds of LR, 17 rounds of L and an impressive 22 rounds of S, a capacity that not only makes the gun ideal for rapid-fire varmint-shooting needs, but also for an enjoyable afternoon's plinking.

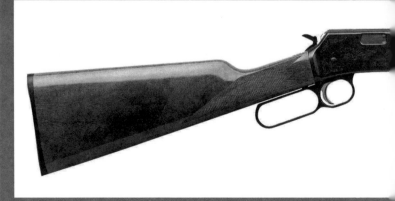

Lever-action guns can be difficult to use if the action is too long, as the gun has to be taken out of the shoulder to accommodate the movement. The lever action on the BL-22, however, is a very short 33 degrees and, as such, the gun would be good for those with small hands, or for those who want a very fast reload to switch quickly between targets without taking the gun from their shoulders. The trigger also moves with the lever to avoid trapped fingers.

The gun (as with all Browning firearms) comes with a trigger lock or other locking attachment. The gun's mechanism also prevents firing of the gun until the lever is swung up to rest, the breech has completely closed and the trigger has been fully released.

Specifications: Browning BL-22 Grade I
Calibre: .22S, .22L, .22LR
Barrel length: 51cm (20in)
Weight: up to 2.27kg (5lb)
Sights: folding leaf rear, bead front
Mechanism: lever action, tubular magazine

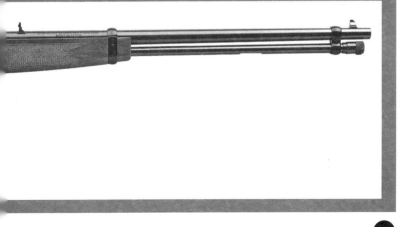

Kneeling Firing Position

A kneeling position creates the opportunity to rest the lead elbow on the knee. The more stable your body structure can be made, the greater your accuracy.

is important is that the position is comfortable and does not create tension in the body while creating a constant relationship between eye and weapon. Circumstances may dictate variations, such as putting the front foot up on a rock or area

of higher ground. Firm footing is important if you want to shoot accurately, but terrain can be used to good advantage. The weapon can be rested on a fence, rock or branch if appropriate, or the front foot can be put up on a support and the lead

elbow rested on the leg for added weapon stability.

Kneeling Firing Position

A kneeling shooting position has the advantages of lower centre of gravity and more points of contact with the ground, both of which promote stability. The lead foot still points at the target, and body alignment is similar to the standing position. The lead leg can be used to support the leading elbow, creating a combat and solid frame to support the weapon.

Sitting Firing Position

A seated position offers good contact with the ground, improving stability. It may not be appropriate in wet and muddy terrain, however.

Do not rest the point of the elbow on the leg; the 'flat of the arm' just behind the elbow is the correct point of contact.

The firing-side foot can be rolled onto its side, in which case you will sit on the side of your foot in a 'low kneeling' position, or you can bend your toes and keep the ball of the foot on the ground. In this 'high kneeling' position you will sit on the back of your foot. Some shooters prefer one over the other; some use both, depending on circumstances – high kneeling is quicker under most circumstances, but some shooters prefer the low position as they feel it is more stable. The lead leg can be extended to lower the front knee and create a rest at an appropriate height.

It is less easy to track moving targets in this position, but it is easier to make use of natural supports. Since the lead arm is supported, vertical variance in shots tends to be less than when using a standing (or 'offhand') shooting position, but the dominant elbow is not supported, so there is more lateral variance than when shooting from a prone position.

Sitting Firing Position
A sitting position offers support to both elbows, and benefits from three points of contact with the ground. However, it does mean putting your buttocks on possibly cold

and/or wet ground, which may not be to your liking. The knees can be drawn up to whatever height is desirable to support both elbows. This position can be comfortable for many shooters, but for older and less flexible people, or those of greater girth, it can be difficult to maintain. One solution is a harness that fits around the legs and helps support them in a shooting position, although this is really not an option if you expect to have to get up and move quickly. Sitting offers concealment from many game creatures, although it can place the sight line unacceptably low in brush. It is a good compromise for game shooting in grassy country, placing the rifle high enough to shoot deer and the like over low obstructions but still increasing accuracy compared with a kneeling or standing position.

Prone Firing Position

The prone position offers the greatest stability, but at the price of taking longer to assume than other shoot-

Prone Firing Position

A prone position is about as stable as a shooter can get. The body is fully supported and cannot move, which would disrupt aim. The lead elbow rests on the ground.

ing positions. It may not always be desirable to lie on your belly, either because of obstructions or wet ground, but this position does enhance accuracy and also offers good concealment. A prone shooting position might be the only option when stalking skittish game that will take off running at the first sign of movement.

A prone position supports both elbows and is relatively easy to maintain, allowing the shooter to rest while waiting for a shot. The natural alignment of rifle and body must be maintained, so the shooting position must be carefully maintained – there is a very limited arc of fire available without crawling around in circles.

A prone position is ideal to make use of a rest of some kind. Some rifles have a built-in bipod or monopod, or one can be improvised. A rucksack or a nearby rock will also make a good rest, and the sling swivel (if one is fitted) can serve, with the fist resting on the ground and gripping the sling to act as rest and elevation mechanism at the

Correct Stance

When firing a longarm, lean forward into the shot, allowing your body weight to brace the recoil. Don't lean back, as this is an unstable position with a poor eyeline down the barrel.

same time. Rests can be used from any position if the height is correct, and some forms of competitive target shooting are specifically about shooting from a rest. Long-range target shooting from a bench is an art all of its own, and has an associated set of techniques. Many of these are similar to those already covered, such as using a sand sock.

Some shooters choose to sit at right angles to the target rather than facing it, cradling the rifle on their arms, which are in turn rested on the bench in an almost folded position. This is a very stable posture, well suited to the sort of minute adjustments needed for 1000m (3280ft) target shooting.

Shotgun Shooting Mechanics

Shotguns are not, in general, particularly precise. A rifled barrel or choke can deliver a slug with a fair degree of accuracy, but this is not the primary application of shotguns. The whole point of birdshot is that it is imprecise; it creates a pattern of shot in the general area a bird might be about to occupy, trading the ability to hit a precise spot for the creation of a 'danger space' that increases the chance of hitting a small, fast-moving target.

When engaging large game with slug or buckshot, the mechanics of shooting a shotgun are much the same as those of using a rifle, but a different technique is required for

fowl, small game like rabbits, and targets that simulate them such as clay pigeons. It may be possible to shoot from a sitting or kneeling position, especially if your approach is stealthy or you have managed to remain concealed and the birds have come close to you. Shooting a sitting duck is precisely what the figure of speech refers to, and is a relatively simple matter.

Most targets, however, have to be tracked. This requires a good, smooth swing of the weapon to a point ahead of the target's line of flight, and a clean follow-through. Stopping the gun at the moment of firing will greatly impair accuracy. Instead, you must follow through after firing and perfecting the swing, which is an important part of shotgun technique.

For some targets, the swing may be at a more or less constant vertical angle, tracking the target horizontally, although no bird is going to make itself easy to hit by flying straight and level just because you want it to. You may have to track the target both vertically and horizontally, chasing the target and overtaking it with your aim point until you are far ahead enough to make the shot.

The mechanics of leading a bird flying horizontally, one coming straight towards the shooter or one climbing fast are broadly similar; the gun must be swung smoothly, but it is necessary to practice all the necessary motions – elevating the

Pull-through Technique

The aim point begins behind the target, and moves along its line of flight a little faster than the bird is moving. The aim point is pulled through the target, and the shot is taken when the aim point has moved just ahead.

A hunter waits behind a tree for game to appear. Trees can provide useful aim supports.

gun requires slightly different body mechanics to traversing it. The two main techniques are 'point and push' or 'pull-through'. For targets that are traveling with constant speed and direction, point and push works well. Here, the shooter tracks the target with the weapon aimed directly at it, gaining a feel for its movement, then 'pushes' the aim point ahead and fires. For targets that are moving more erratically or which appear suddenly, it is better to track the target from behind, overtake it and then shoot when the aim point has moved ahead. This is termed pull-through, which describes the way the aim point is dragged through the target and ahead of it.

Estimating lead is a critical part of shotgun technique, and here there is no substitute for practice. Clay pigeon shooting is excellent training for hunting as well as a fun sport in its own right. A shotgunner needs to learn how much to lead a target that is flying at any given angle relative to his position and at a range of speeds, and clay pigeons are a much more reliable source of targets than wild birds.

Many shotguns have only the most rudimentary of sights, often just a bead on the muzzle. This is generally sufficient, since a lot of shotgunning is a matter of look-

and-shoot, with lead and aim point estimated by eye. This ability can only be gained by practice, but there are some fundamental errors that can be avoided.

One problem a lot of shooters have when hunting is being distracted by multiple targets, especially when several birds are flying in close proximity. Any tendency to shoot at the flock as a whole must be curbed; there is more air than bird in even a dense flock, so the only way a hit will occur is by accident. Instead, it is necessary to pick a single bird as the target and stick to it, even if leading it takes the aim point close to another target. Flitting between targets does not permit good shooting, but even if this is not done, it is possible to become distracted and make a poor shot. Again, the art of eliminating other targets and focusing on just one is something that can only be gained by practice.

The way the gun is brought to the shoulder is critical to making a good shot, but many shooters do not practise this essential skill. The gun must be brought from its resting position to the shoulder in a smooth and quick, but not hurried, movement. It must be pulled in to the shoulder as the target is acquired, allowing a smooth swing and follow-through unimpaired by last-second fiddling with the gun position.

Many shots are taken at targets that appear quite suddenly, so the whole process of taking the shot, from first spotting the target and deciding that the shot is worth taking, through shouldering the gun and tracking the target to the moment of firing, is all part of hitting the target. It must all be done right and as part of a whole. If each part of the process is perfect, but there are jerks and gaps between them, then the end product will be a miss.

Lock Time

The firing mechanism of a weapon used to be called a lock (e.g. matchlock, wheel-lock, flintlock), and the term 'lock time' refers to the delay between pulling the trigger and the weapon discharging. Modern weapons have a rather shorter lock time than those that had to move a length of slow-match into contact with a pile of gunpowder and hope it caught fire, but there is still a delay between choosing to shoot and the weapon discharging.

Ruger Gold Label

Weight reduction is the main focus of the Gold Label. The barrels are made from lightweight metal and the extremely shallow receiver is constructed of stainless steel – resulting in a gun that only weighs 3kg (6.6lb). The interchangeable chokes also have very thin walls, and the gun comes with a five-choke set (these are ranged from Skeet to Full), so the shooter can set the pattern according to their particular style of shooting or hunting. The chokes are also fine for shooting with steel shot, so can be used in environmentally sensitive areas (typically wetlands) or in countries where lead shot is banned (i.e. most of the European Union).

Although a very light gun, the Gold Label is chambered for 76mm (3in) magnum cartridges – recoil must be quite firm when firing heavy shot loads. Only a 71cm (28in) barrel length is available, and this has a full-length rib with a simple bead sight at the muzzle end. The woodwork is American walnut, and the stock

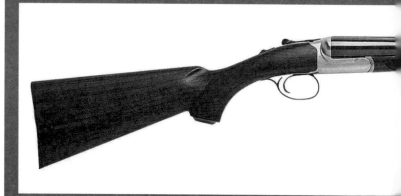

is available either with a classic straight neck or with a pistol-grip configuration. The fore-end is of the splinter type, and the weight of the gun balances at the junction of fore-end and receiver. An auto-safety reduces the risk of an accident in the field, and the safety switch is combined with the barrel selector. Shooting reviews of the Gold Label have been very favourable, noting the gun's natural 'pointability' and its ease of transportation.

Specifications: Ruger Gold Label
Gauge/calibre: 12
Barrel length: 71cm (28in)
Weight: 3kg (6.6lb)
Ejector type: automatic ejectors
Chokes: interchangeable

Target practice is necessary to become a good shot with any weapon, but in some cases target shooting is the point of the exercise. Seeing who is the best shot with a given weapon (or with a weapon of their own choice) over a given distance can be a source of casual amusement or serious competition that takes someone all the way to the Olympic Games.

Firing Ranges

Formal firing ranges are designed with safety in mind, with a good solid backstop and usually obstructions to the sides to prevent wildly bad shots from endangering anyone. Ranges also have solid safety procedures in place and usually a range master or safety officer who is responsible for ensuring that no one gets hurt. The instructions of the safety officer overrule everything else – unless he says it is safe to shoot, then it is not safe to shoot, no matter who thinks he is being too fussy.

Ranges generally have a set of rules that are partly etiquette and partly safety procedures. On some ranges it is acceptable to carry weapons holstered behind the firing line, and in some it is not. Many ranges have a hard and fast rule

....

The Anschutz Model 1417 is an ideal lightweight gun for hunting varmints.

4

Target shooting can be practice for other sports, or an event in itself. It is a lot more effective to learn to shoot on a range and then go hunting than to plunge into the wilderness without prior experience.

Target Pistols and Rifles

Eyes and Ears

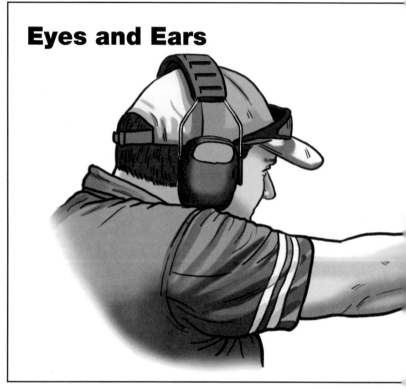

that every gun must be on a table, magazine out and action open, before anyone is permitted to move ahead of the firing line. In many cases, shooters are expected to move out of booths or away from their weapons before the call is made that the range is clear, and not to go back until the safety officer calls that it is clear to shoot.

Rules of this sort can become habit, but occasionally people

get distracted and break them for innocent reasons. Ducking back into a shooting booth for a forgotten item, or to get out of the rain, should not pose a hazard to anyone – but the safety officer cannot know that you will not do something stupid. Consequences can range from a reminder about the rules to being banned from the range – although that tends only to happen after persistent infractions.

This shooter has got it only half right – his ears are properly defended but his glasses are protecting only the logo on his hat, which is not really the best use for them.

firearm. Despite the tongue-in-cheek nature of the notice, the fact that it is necessary to warn shooters about both doing what they are not supposed to, and making spurious excuses about it, suggests that some range users may not have been good-mannered about it.

A near-obsession with safety and other rules can be a bit of a pain, but it is the only way to be sure that accidents do not occur. In a smaller and less formal shooting environment, the same sort of rules should be observed. It is worth agreeing on a single person to be responsible for safety before engaging in any sort of shooting, even just a bit of fun plinking. Indeed, it is when shooting becomes casual that mistakes are made. Complacency is dangerous around firearms, and is actually more likely when just having fun than when in a more serious or formal shooting environment.

'Plinking'

Fun target shooting is known as 'plinking'. Almost any handgun will do for this purpose, although the better the quality of the gun, the more accurate the outcome. Some shooters purchase reproduction historical weapons and the like as novelty 'fun guns'; many of these are fine, accurate weapons but their appeal is aesthetic as much as practical.

Plinking in this manner is recreational, i.e. it is about having a

Other rules may be about good manners as much as anything else. I have read with amusement what amounts to an open letter to shooters from a range owner in California. A sign deals with the habit of some shooters of firing at the metal drums holding up the range marker flags, suggesting that anyone claiming to have hit one 'by accident' is essentially stating that they are too incompetent to be allowed near a

Weatherby Mk V Compact

bit of fun and not being too serious about it – although there are those who festoon their weapons with all manner of gadgets and accessories before putting a few holes in tin cans. There is nothing wrong with this at all; for some shooters it is part of the fun. However, blasting cans with an accessorized combat handgun is a bit beyond the realms of 'serious' sport shooting.

To keep down the costs of recreational shooting, common small calibres such as .22LR, .32 or .380 are popular. Plinking is an excellent way to introduce a new shooter to the sport, or to stay in practice, and there is really no need for a powerful gun. Obviously, if the purpose is to practise shooting for self-defence, then at some point you will need to practise with the actual weapon you intend to use, but a bit of target practice with any firearm helps maintain a good standard of marksmanship.

Competitive Target Shooting

There is a lot to be said for shooting

Essentially a Weatherby Mk V rifle turned into a big handgun, the Mk V Compact is somewhat lighter and easier to carry than a rifle, but still has the accuracy and punch of a rifle round.

just for the satisfaction of hitting the target, but once things get competitive, then the challenge is usually to create a tighter group, to hit a smaller target than someone else or to get more shots on target in a given time. The search for new ways of competing with one another has led to the creation of some quite unique gun sports.

The most common target shooting events are those where the firer shoots from a fixed station at either static or moving ('running') targets. In some events, such as those

recognized by the ISSF (International Shooting Sport Federation), the time taken is not a factor, only the quality of the shot. A target marked in concentric rings gives a shore of 1 to 10 points (or 0 for a miss) on each shot, with the shooter's total being compared to that of others.

Events of this sort are competed over various ranges, including short-range air rifle events and low-powered rifles firing over reduced ranges to simulate a more powerful weapon over several hundred metres. Shooting with rifles may be

Browning Buck Mark

The Browning Buck Mark has one of the most unusual appearances of any auto-loading rifle, as it actually is a rifle redesign of Browning's Buck Mark pistol. The Buck Mark pistol is a popular .22LR 10-shot auto handgun for target shooting or light hunting. Its rifle counterpart retains the same blowback-action mechanism, blowback generally being a reliable and relatively inexpensive method of auto-loading. The Buck Mark pistol becomes a rifle through two principal changes. A walnut or laminated hardwood stock is fitted to the back of the gun on metal braces that extend from the rear of the receiver and the bottom of the pistol grip. At the other end of the gun, there is an obvious change in barrel configuration. Two different 46cm (18in) barrels are available for the Buck Mark. The first is the tapered sporter-weight barrel for the Sporter models. For Target models, there is a heavy steel bull or alloy-sleeved barrel. The crowns of all the barrels are recessed; this shields them from damage that could impair accuracy.

Because it has pistol grip along with a full fore-end, the Buck Mark handles somewhere between a pistol and a rifle. Its accuracy, however, is not in doubt. The Sporter model has a Truglo/Marble's adjustable fibre-optic sight for quick target acquisition, and the guns can take scopes via an integral rail scope mount. The design also means that the shooter has an extremely light weapon, with the Sporter versions weighing only 1.9kg (4.1lb) while the Target guns are a little heavier at around 2.4kg (5.25lb). As such the Buck Mark rifle allows for the very quick acquisition of targets and, with its 10-round detachable box magazine, for quick shooting.

Specifications: Browning Buck Mark Semi-Automatic Rifle
Calibre: .22LR
Barrel length: 46cm (18in)
Weight: up to 2.4kg (5.25lb)
Sights: fibre-optic sights; rail mounting for scope
Mechanism: blowback operated

Plinking Targets

Virtually any object can be used as a target for plinking, but some shooters like to set up targets that will swing or flip when hit, giving visual confirmation of a good shot.

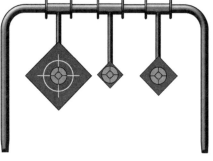

from different positions – standing, kneeling or prone. Some events, typically long-range competitions, allow the shooter to fire from a bench rest. These events require an extremely accurate weapon, which may not be optimized for other forms of shooting.

Types of Target Pistols

Ladies Sport

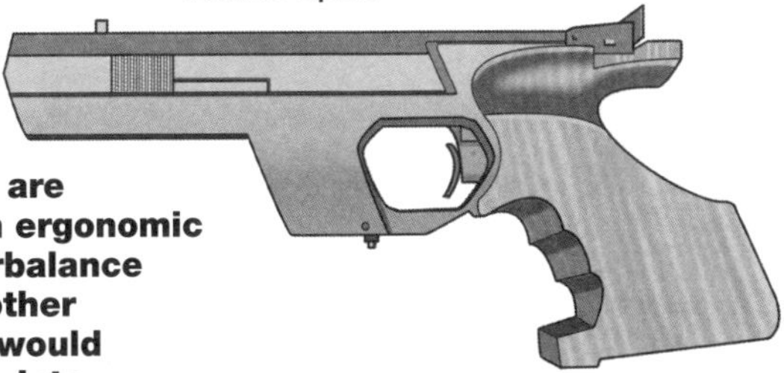

Target pistols are designed with ergonomic grips, counterbalance weights and other features that would not be appropriate on a weapon that was going to be carried in the field.

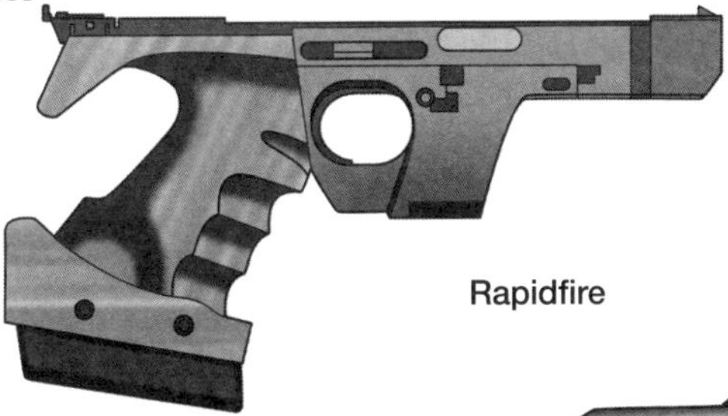

Rapidfire

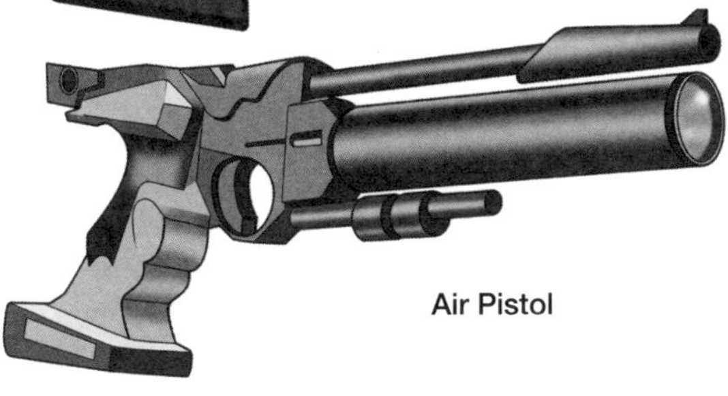

Air Pistol

There are many variations on the theme of target shooting, some of them resulting from local legislation. In the UK, gallery rifle shooting, using rifles chambered for pistol cartridges, has become popular since the private ownership of handguns was outlawed. Other events simulate

Set Target

Target rings provide a simple way to score a shooting contest. Holes can be patched with stickers or the target replaced for the next round.

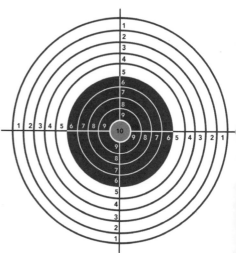

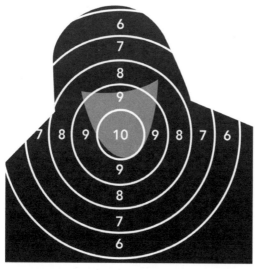

hunting conditions in the country of origin, or are derived from other historical precedents. Service Rifle competitions are open only to current or previous military service rifles, while an 'across the course' event requires the shooter to fire from standing, kneeling and prone positions at various points.

Biathlon

In some cases shooting is combined with a different discipline to create a unique challenge. In the biathlon, competitors must ski a course, stopping to shoot targets from a standing or prone position. Depending on the rules in force, the competitor suffers either a time penalty or must ski an extra distance for every missed shot. The combination of hard physical effort and shooting makes this event particularly challenging; a shooter who is breathing hard from getting to the firing point fast may miss, which will undo the good work he has done so far and require additional effort to make up time... which may cause another miss at the next shooting station.

A variant on the biathlon theme is the 'summer biathlon' in which the skiing component is replaced by running. The standard biathlon uses a 20km (12.4-mile) course, although there are several variants with a shorter course and a pursuit version in which the competitors begin the

Sako TRG 22

The TRG 22 is a pure accuracy weapon designed for either police officers or those wanting the most exacting competition standards in target sports. It has an arresting appearance. The composite stock is deeply cut down over the wrist, and the adjustability of the weapon is evident – the comb is adjustable for drop and cast and the butt plate is extendable to alter the length of pull. The stock material itself is a hard-wearing, weather-impervious composite, and the barrel has a completely free-floating arrangement in relation to the fore-end.

The TRG 22 is capable of pinpoint accuracy up to 300m (984ft), but is capable of decent groupings well beyond this range. It is chambered solely for the redoubtable .308 Win (also known as the 7.62x51 NATO) and it has a large (for a centrefire bolt-action rifle) magazine capacity of 10 rounds. Target-grade barrels are cold-hammer-forged, and these can be provided with a mirage-sling fitting to obscure heat radiation.

The three-lug bolt is particularly precise in feeding the rounds from the centreline of the magazine, and moving the bolt handle through only 60 degrees of turn operates the gun. Triggers can be adjusted for the pull-weight preference of the individual shooter. Naturally, there are no fixed sights, but the gun's 17mm (0.7in) rails will take all manner of professional scopes for either military or target shooting.

Specifications: Sako TRG 22
Calibre: .308 Win (7.62x51 NATO)
Barrel length: 66cm (26in)
Weight: average 4.7kg (10.25lb)
Sights: rails for scope mounting
Mechanism: bolt action, magazine fed

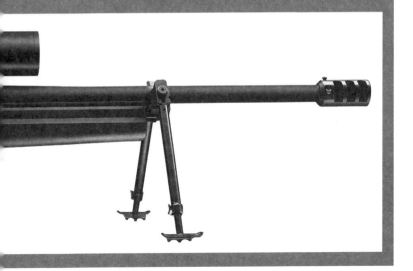

Winter Biathlon

In the Winter Biathlon, shooters must not only shoot after the exertion of fast ski-ing, but must also shoot while standing on skis.

course at intervals determined by a previous event. In this case it is not time that matters – the winner is the first to pass the finishing post.

The biathlon rifle is chambered for .22LR ammunition, with shots taken at a 50m (164ft) range. There are five targets to be hit, and missing each one imposes either a 1-minute or 150m (492ft) penalty on the competitor. This is an extremely challenging event, requiring the

competitor to juggle shooting and skiing ability with a tactical sense of when to push hard and when to slow down and try to reduce heart rate and breathing for a better chance at hitting the targets.

Some forms of competition are designed to simulate combat rather than hunting, and are often termed 'practical' events, e.g. practical shotgun. The usual format is for the competitor to run a course, starting with the weapon holstered in the case of handguns, engaging a series of targets at each station along the way. Penalties are incurred for misses or, in some cases, for hitting 'no-shoot' targets. Scoring is a mix of time and hits, with the shooter's points per second ratio being compared to those of other competitors.

Scoring can be complex, often requiring two or more valid hits on each target and with more points for greater accuracy. The power of the weapon used is also a factor; more potent weapons score more points for the same hit, although a bullseye always gets maximum points. This reflects the greater knockdown power of more potent weapons, which is relevant in a practical competition, and trades off against the greater difficulty of shooting well with powerful guns.

Other Shooting Competitions

At the top end of practical shooting the field is open to all weapons, although medium-calibre handguns chambered for 9mm are popular. Sighting aids such as laser pointers and large-capacity magazines are permitted, whereas in other divisions they may not be. In some ways these accessories may not be in keeping with the 'practical' origins of the competition – handguns are normally carried as light, handy sidearms, and

fitting them with several accessories and an oversized magazine might take them out of the combat/sidearm field. In this way, the handguns used in top-end practical pistol events are every bit as specialized as those used by Olympic target shooters.

There are practical pistol competitions geared to various types of weapons, such as revolver-only events or competitions where only versions of the traditional M1911 .45 semi-automatic pistol are permitted. The standard division is geared towards the sort of handguns typically carried for self-defence, without much in the way of accessories. An event of this sort would be winnable with a gun bought for home defence or a police sidearm, which is to a great extent the point of the competition. Indeed, there are police-only competitions designed to improve law enforcement shooting techniques; these are not open to the public.

Three-gun Event

A variant of the practical shooting competition is the three-gun event, in which the competitors run a course where they must engage a range of targets with a rifle, a shotgun and a handgun. This kind of event requires a certain amount of mental gear-shifting to encompass the different skills required, and has a number of specialized techniques associated with it. Some critics of

Walther KK 300

The Walther name has been synonymous with high-quality European firearms since the early part of the 20th century, and the KK 300 is a top-end target rifle for superlative competition performance.

Walther has been particularly well known for its military outputs, particularly its famous PP/PPK pistol. Its hi-tech weapons today include the G22 semi-automatic rifle and the P22 and P99 semi-automatic handguns, plus a wide range of target air rifles, air pistols and small-bore rifles. The KK 300 rifle has adjustability at every level of its construction – competition shooters customize their weapons until they are the perfect body fit.

There are three different sizes of pistol grip (the KK 300 has a true pistol grip rather than being part of the flow of the stock). The stock itself is adjustable for every conceivable dimension and comfort, including drop, cast, length of pull and shoulder fit. A hook arm provides stability for various disciplines, and the gun can be set up for prone, kneeling or free-standing disciplines. All the settings can be locked in place for easy setup at a competition.

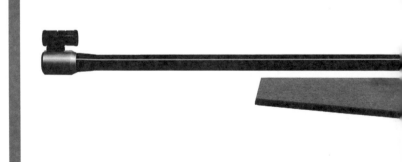

The KK 300 is a small-bore competition rifle in the .22LR calibre. The trigger and action in particular have been designed for a light pull and an incredibly fast lock time. Trigger pull is fully adjustable, the range being 70–130g (2.5–4.6oz). The length of the match-grade barrel comes to 65cm (25.5in) and the total weight is 5.9kg (13lb).

Specifications: Walther KK 300
Calibre: .22LR
Barrel length: 65cm (25.5in)
Weight: 5.9kg (13lb)
Sights: aperture rear sight and front post
Mechanism: bolt action

Cowboy Action Shooting

Cowboy Action Shooting events are more about spectacle and fun than perfect shooting, but that does not mean that the participants don't take their messing about seriously.

three-gun events suggest that these 'competition tricks' take the sport away from its origins as a test of

practical combat shooting ability and may promote habits that would be a liability in a real gunfight. This,

however, is the inevitable effect of creating a competition – competitors will play to the rules in order to win, and if those rules do not perfectly reflect reality, then neither will the actions of the competitors.

Winchester Model 1885

Emblazoned with the Winchester motif, the Winchester 1885 High Wall Hunter has been chambered in a number of calibres over the years. Its single-shot, falling-block design has proved extremely reliable.

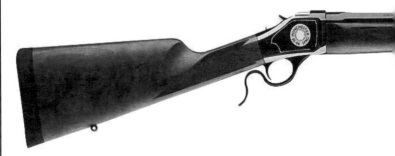

Cowboy Action Shooting

One form of competition straddles the line between re-enactment, competitive shooting and having fun with guns. Collectively known as Cowboy Action Shooting, these events recapture the (real or imagined) spirit of the Old West. Competitors are limited to weapons that were available up to just after the end of the 19th century, and are required to dress as cowboys or other Western figures, and in some events spurs are mandatory. There is a variant based on the *Wild Bunch* movie that allows military dress from the period, and some slightly later firearms,

but the spirit is the same. In many events, competitors run a course tackling targets with revolver, rifle and shotgun, and are expected to shoot in a manner true to the spirit of the movies made about the era – whatever the reality may have been. Thus revolvers are carried with five rounds only chambered, as was the practice before modern safety devices were introduced, and targets are engaged with the gun in one hand only. It is, however, permissible to use a revolver in each hand.

The courses are set up to reflect a Western story, involving bank robberies, shootouts with outlaws

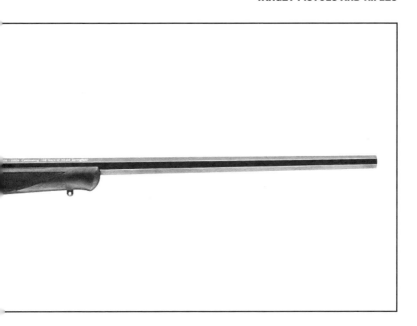

and similar Western movie tropes. The course is timed, with penalties for missing some of the targets and other infractions of the course rules.

The Western movie theme is expanded upon by other events, such as mounted shooting. For safety reasons, the competitor's gun is loaded with blanks, which are still sufficiently powerful to burst balloon targets as he rides through the course on horseback. This is a fairly specialized skillset, but not quite so exotic as some of those on display. Some competitors will give displays of skill reminiscent of the 'Wild West shows' of the early 20th century, including making trick shots while

juggling with live guns. This sort of thing is as hair-raisingly dangerous as it sounds for most people, but it does make an impressive spectacle.

Some Cowboy Action Shooting events do require the use of percussion-cap weapons, but in most cases it is sufficient to use replica late-period weapons firing unitary cartridges. There are various rules about what weapons can be used in which events, and in some cases clothing must match the chosen weapon. All this adds up to a form of competition that is geared towards having fun as much as winning, but which is nevertheless fiercely contested.

Henry Big Boy

The Henry rifle is embedded in the history of the early United States, and the Henry Repeating Arms Company has revisited this history in its series of Big Boy lever-action guns. The Henry Big Boy is so named after its calibres. While Henry's Golden Boy lever-action rifles are in various .22 and .17 calibres, and so meet the needs of varmint hunters, the Big Boy range is in .44 Magnum, .45 Colt and .357 Magnum. These calibres make the Big Boy a serious rifle. Henry's website describes three particular groups who might be interested in the Big Boy: Wild West history enthusiasts, those who involve themselves in Cowboy Action Shooting and big-game hunters.

The modern-day Henry Company has invested the Big Boy with historical authenticity. It has a 51cm (20in) octagonal barrel and a solid brass receiver. The latter, as Henry points out, means that the Big Boy 'is the first American made .44 Henry lever action featuring a solid brass receiver since the original Henry rifle of 1860'. (A brass barrel band and a brass butt plate are also standard features.)

A tubular magazine holds 10 of the .44 Mag rounds, giving the Big Boy serious game-shooting power. Press reviews of the Big

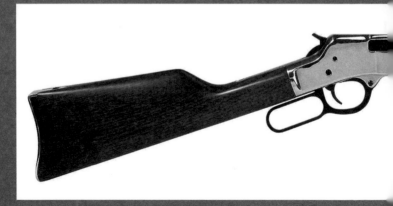

Boy have noted how smooth and reliable the action is, with positive loading through an easy flick of the under-lever. Ejection is via a side port. Loading the Big Boy involves removing the brass loading tube, dropping in the rounds and then replacing the tube. Sights on the Big Boy consist of an adjustable marble semi-buckhorn rear sight with white diamond insert and brass beaded front sight. These sights give a good level of accuracy to around 50m (164ft). There are no scope mountings on the receiver, but Henry also sells cantilever scope mounts.

Specifications: Henry Big Boy
Calibre: .357 Mag, .44 Mag, .45 Colt
Barrel length: 51cm (20in)
Weight: 3.9kg (8.68lb)
Sights: open
Mechanism: lever action, magazine fed

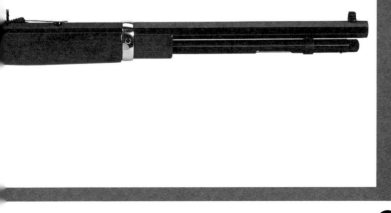

Clay pigeon shooting – perhaps more accurately referred to as 'clay target shooting' since some targets represent creatures other than birds – can be used as training for hunting, a fun way to spend an afternoon once in a while or an utterly serious sporting contest. It is one of the disciplines in the Olympic Games.

The sport started out using live birds released from a trap when the shooters were ready, but for many decades now the target has been a clay disc projected from a device known as a trap. Traps vary in construction; some use a manually loaded, cocked and released spring, while others are very sophisticated. Some traps can hold hundreds of clays and release them in rapid sequence, although normally clays are launched one or two at a time.

Most targets are launched through the air to simulate birds in flight, although some (known as 'rabbits') are rolled along the ground. Clays differ in design but there are standard sizes for competition. Various designs create different flight characteristics, but what most clays have in common is that their flight path is predictable – unlike the birds they represent.

....

Clay shooting can be enjoyed by anyone, from an amateur with an inexpensive gun, all the way to Olympic competitors. There are events at every level of ability.

5

Clay Pigeon Shooting can be a good way to practise hunting birds, but many clay shooters have never gone hunting and have no desire to do so. It has become a popular sport in its own right.

Clay Pigeon Shooting

Clay Trap

A clay trap flings the target into the air. It generates sufficient force to be almost as dangerous as the guns the shooters are using, and is subject to strict safety rules.

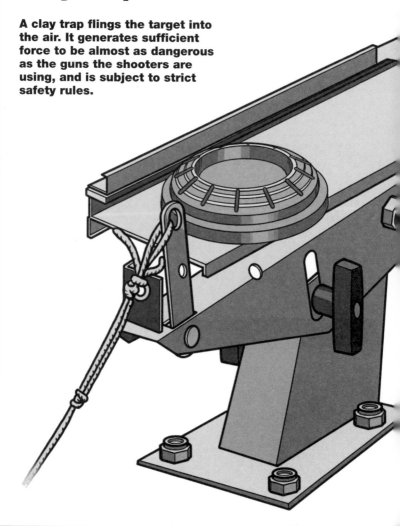

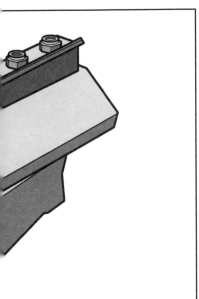

A clay pigeon comes out of the trap with a certain amount of energy and in a given direction. It gradually loses that energy due to air resistance, and so tends to slow down and drop in a manner that quickly becomes predictable to an experienced shooter. By contrast, birds can change direction and accelerate in flight, making them rather less simple to track. One type of clay target is designed to fly unpredictably, creating a rather more realistic shooting experience, but for many shooters this is irrelevant – clay target shooting is enjoyed by thousands of people who would never even consider firing at any living thing, and has become a highly respected sport in its own right.

At its most basic, clay pigeon shooting requires little more than a trap, a means to activate it and a gun. The shooter calls 'pull' to indicate that he is ready to shoot, and a clay is released by the trap operator. Even at this most basic level, clay shooting does require a fair amount of skill, but a beginner with a good instructor can start achieving hits on a first session – providing fairly easy shots are set up.

Competitive Clay Pigeon Shooting

For more advanced shooters, and for competitive purposes, the task is made harder in various ways, and different styles of competition have their own names.

Benelli SuperSport

The SuperSport is an inertia-cycled gun. On firing, the gun recoils and the floating bolt compresses an inertia spring. This inertia spring then drives the bolt backwards to eject the spent cartridge and re-cock the mechanism before the bolt is pushed forward to the locked position by a recoil spring. The advantage of this system is its durability, reliability and its scope for coping with the most potent of cartridges. Yet as well as handling the magnum cartridges, the gun will also cycle perfectly well on light 24g (just under 1oz) competition loads.

Chevron-shaped cut-outs in the stock are a visual signature of the ComfortTech recoil-reduction system. As we have already seen with the Black Eagle, this system, which operates through a controlled flexing of the stock, reduces both felt recoil and muzzle flip to give better second-target acquisition. This is particularly important for clay shooters, when the second of a fast simultaneous pair can be lost if the shooter has to ride out an excessive recoil before dropping back onto the second bird. As a further limit on muzzle flip and recoil, the SuperSport has a ported barrel, which vents gas out from the sides of the muzzle.

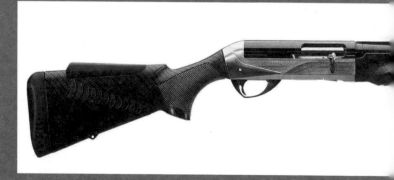

Because of its declared purpose as a clay-shooting gun, the SuperSport is provided with extended CrioChoke interchangeable choke tubes. Benelli claims that 'When it comes to smoking targets, the SuperSport's Crio barrel and CrioChokes produce patterns 13.2 per cent more dense than other brands'. Reviews in shooting magazines seem to bear out the claims, with one reviewer stating that with Improved Cylinder a '20-yard rabbit was turned to dust' (*Clay Shooting*, October 2005). Some sporting shooters might, therefore, feel shy about using the tighter chokes. In summary, the Benelli occupies the summit of semi-automatic technology, and will happily take on the most demanding clay grounds.

Specifications: Benelli SuperSport
Gauge/calibre: 12
Barrel length: 71cm (28in), 76cm (30in)
Weight (76cm/30in barrel): 3.3kg (7.3lb)
Mechanism: inertia operated
Chokes: interchangeablemechanism; blowback operated

Sporting Clays

Clay shooting venues are set up for comfort as well as safety. The side barriers will halt an overzealous swing of the gun before anyone is endangered.

The three main forms of clay pigeon shooting are known as trap shooting, skeet shooting and sporting clays. In most forms of trap shooting there is a single launch point (or 'house') for targets, although their trajectory can vary considerably. Some targets are thrown as doubles, i.e. two clays are projected simultaneously and diverge in flight.

Trap Shooting

The most popular form of trap shooting in the United States is, predictably perhaps, called American Trap Shooting. The standard format is to have five firing stations behind the trap house and for each competitor to shoot at five targets launched singly. The trap house prevents the shooter seeing the position of the trap and thus predicting the trajectory of the target. A 'doubles' event varies in that the trap does not alter its trajectory but launches two clays at once, which causes them to take different paths. A handicapped event requires skilled shooters to take a position further away from the house.

In the UK and countries influenced by traditional British shooting, Down-the-Line is the most popular variant of trap shooting. In this case the shooter is allowed to take two shots at the target, with more points scored for a first-shot hit than for a second-barrel kill.

The Olympic version of trapshooting uses 15 houses, each of which is fixed on a set trajectory, rather than the more usual single-buy variable machine. Shooters know they will get a fixed set of shots – 10 coming from each side and five moving away from the shooter – but the order is randomized so that the shooter cannot know what is to come next. In the course of a round, each competitor thus takes exactly the same shots as everyone else, cycling through the five firing stations as he goes.

Another variant of trap shooting is variously called 'universal trench', 'five trap' or 'universal trap' and has five traps set to launch along different trajectories in a trench in front of the shooters. The shooter cannot predict where the target will emerge, making this a challenging discipline.

Skeet Shooting

Skeet shooting uses two trap houses with different trajectories. In the course of an event the shooter cycles through seven shooting stations, tackling a total of 25 targets that are a mix of single and double releases. A simple one-point-per-hit system is used. The Olympic version of skeet shooting incorporates a variable delay between the shooter's call for a target and the actual release, to prevent the competitor from calling for a target and firing at the place he knows it will be.

Sporting Clays

Sporting clays is the most varied and variable form of clay pigeon shooting.

Trap Shooting Layout

In competitive trap shooting, the competitors cycle through several firing positions, ensuring that everyone shoots from each position. Advanced shooters can be handicapped by using a more distant shooting position.

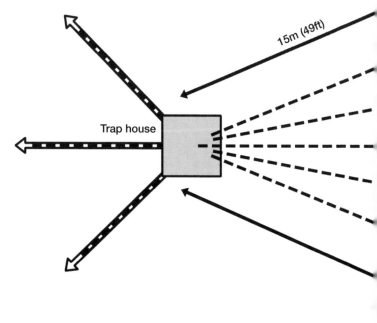

15m (49ft)

Trap house

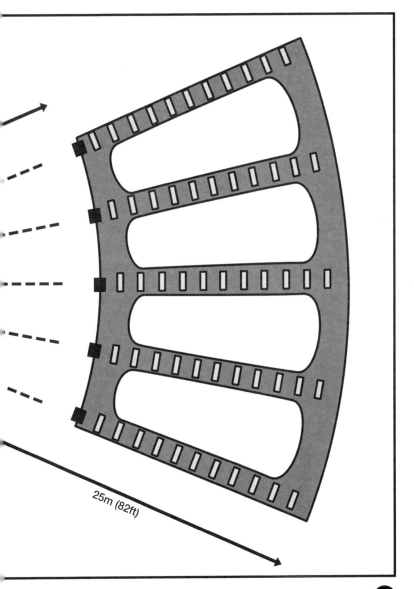

25m (82ft)

Skeet Shooting – Field Layout

In skeet shooting, competitors have to cope with low and high targets, although their trajectory will be predictable.

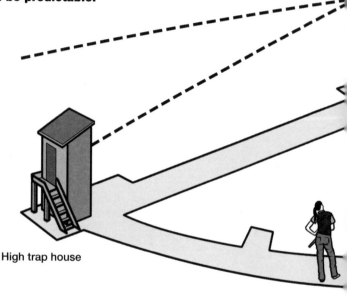

High trap house

A sporting clays course is designed to simulate hunting conditions, and shooters may have to contend with targets coming from all angles, including high overhead and rolling along the ground. Rather than standing at one station or cycling through a line, a squad of shooters move through a course containing anywhere from 10 to 15 traps. At each trap there will be several targets, which may appear singly or in doubles. Doubles are variable – they may be thrown simultaneously or one

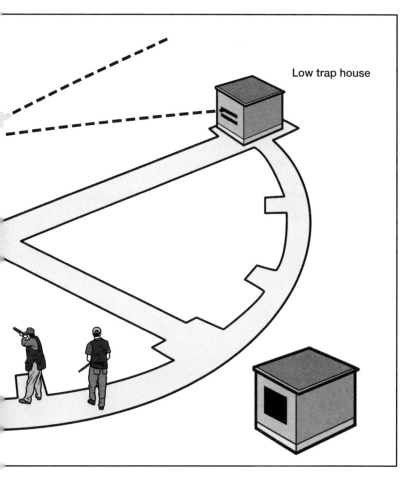

Low trap house

after the other, or the second may be launched at the sound of the shot.

Guns for Clay Pigeon Shooting

The standard gun for clay shooting, in so far as one exists, is a 12-gauge shotgun. Some shooters prefer 20-gauge, which has similar characteristics but lighter recoil, and these two gauges are by far the most commonly used. It does not require much impact to break a clay but they are fairly hard to hit, so lighter shot

Side-by-side Shotgun

Side-by-side shotguns are more traditional than over-under designs, and are still insisted upon by some purists who consider anyone with an over-under to be some kind of cowboy.

is generally used. For competitive shooting there are restrictions on the weight of shot that can be selected, and in some cases home-loaded shells are not permitted.

Single Shot vs. Double Barrel

Single-shot guns can be used for clay shooting, but they are favoured mainly by advanced shooters who relish the additional challenge of only having one shell. The felt recoil on a single-barrelled gun is heavier than a double-barrelled weapon or one that has a magazine under the barrel, which can be a consideration when shooting all day.

A double-barrelled gun also has the advantage of allowing a rapid second shot. Traditionalists may prefer a side-by-side design but the typical sporting gun is an over-under configuration. Stacking the barrels vertically makes aiming more instinctive than with a traditional gun, although it is worth noting that even on an over-under gun the barrels may not be perfectly parallel and the aim point of each may vary. Nevertheless, this is the best choice as a starting gun for clay shooting, and may remain the best choice even in top-end condition.

In Olympic clay pigeon shooting there are requirements that the weapon be visibly unloaded and the action open during transit to and from some of the shooting stations. This imposes a greater delay with a magazine-equipped gun than a break-action over-under, ensuring that the double-barrelled gun remains a firm favourite with competitors everywhere.

In areas where guns are heavily controlled, it is generally easier to get a licence for a double-barrelled weapon, and there is also far less mechanical complexity with a breech-loaded shotgun than a magazine-fed one. That said, pump-action and semi-automatic shotguns are popular choices in some areas. Both have the advantage that the magazine can

Recoil

It is wise to be sensible about how much recoil you can handle. Some powerful guns kick very hard and can cause injury, especially if they are not held properly, and you are not likely to shoot well with a gun that you are frightened of or cannot control properly. Hitting the target with a lighter gun is more likely to win you respect than endlessly missing with some sort of monster cannon.

Semi-automatic Shotgun

Semi-automatic shotguns allow quick follow-up shots. The action of the weapon absorbs some of the recoil, helping the shooter to stay on target.

contain several shells, although there is rarely time for repeated shots at the same clay.

Pump-action vs. Semi-Automatics

A pump-action shotgun can be used for clay shooting; indeed, in terms of actually shooting at the clays, it really matters little what sort of weapon the shot comes out of. A pump-action weapon has a single barrel, meaning that there can be no difference in aim point between shots. At least, none caused by the weapon itself. A second shot with a double-barrelled weapon is simply a matter of shooting again, but with a pump-action gun it requires taking the weapon off target, chambering a new round by working the slide and then re-acquiring the target before firing again. All this has to be accomplished in a very limited time and while it is quite possible, the requirement to take the gun off target reduces accuracy.

Thus pump-action guns are not really ideal for clay shooting, although if you do not intend trying to make a second shot at any given target, then one is as good as any other gun. Semi-automatic shotguns, on the other hand, are well suited. A semi-automatic shotgun has the same advantages as a pump-action gun but does not need to be taken off target while the next shell is chambered. This allows two (or even

Clay Competitions

Beginner shooters will miss more often than not, which can be wasteful of clays. Sometimes it is acceptable for a more experienced shooter to take a shot after the beginner if they do not make a hit.

Beretta AL391 Teknys

The Teknys is one of Beretta's most advanced sporting guns. A gas-operated semi-automatic gun, it is an advanced firearm suited to both sporting clays and field shooting, and a weapon that is known for its reliability. The gas-operated mechanism installed in the Teknys is a sophisticated but still dependable system. Its variable-gas system utilizes just enough of the propellant gas to cycle the action, and the remaining gas is expelled via ports in the underside of the fore-end. The mechanism can handle a wide range of loads, and the gun is chambered for up to 76mm (3in) magnum cartridges.

Many people choose auto-loaders specifically for the soft recoil (much of the recoil on any semi-automatic is taken by the return spring). All Teknys guns are fitted with a Gel-Tek recoil pad, a soft pad that squashes under impact and so reduces the amount of shock transferred to the shooter's shoulder and also deadens recoil vibrations (the pads can be changed easily). At the shooter's request, however, a further spring-mass recoil-reduction system can be added into the stock.

Semi-automatics can be prey to corrosion in a way that breech-loaders are not: the piston and related parts are subject to the corrosive firing gases, and water ingressing through the ejection

port can work its way throughout the mechanism. Beretta produces any metal parts that come into contact with gas in corrosion-resistant inox (stainless) steel and supplement this with further protective treatments.

The wood parts are also coated with Beretta's patented X-tra Wood finish, this giving a varnish-like depth to the wood grain while also being totally waterproof.

The more subtle features of the Teknys attest to its suitability as both a clay and a field gun. The trigger guard is enlarged to take glove-clad fingers for winter shooters. A luminous Truglo front sight stands out clearly in poor light conditions. The Optima-Bore barrels, which have lengthened forcing cones, and the extended Optimachoke Plus choke tubes keep the shot patterns dense and even.

Specifications: Beretta AL391 Teknys
Gauge/calibre: 12, 20
Barrel length (12 gauge): 61cm (24in), 66cm (26in), 71cm (28in), 76cm (30in)
Weight: 3kg (6.6lb)
Mechanism: gas operated
Chokes: Optimachoke Plus interchangeable

several) quick shots to be taken without disturbing the aim point.

Another advantage of semi-automatics is the reduction in felt recoil. Since some of the recoil energy from each shot is absorbed by the mechanism and used to chamber the next shell, less is transferred to the shooter. A semi-automatic is also a good choice if you intend to use it for hunting, as it will absorb the recoil of heavier shells better.

In theory there is no reason why you cannot shoot clays with a 'combat' type shotgun, complete with detachable magazine, but this might be frowned upon by fellow shooters who take their sport a bit more seriously and expect others to use 'appropriate' guns. However, more than likely your clay-shooting gun will be a more conventional tubular-magazine type. Ironically, it is perhaps easier to put your weapon in a visibly safe condition if you can remove the magazine.

Semi-automatic shotguns did at one time have a reputation for unreliability, which continues to hang around despite the fact that modern guns are vastly more reliable than the early semi-automatics that were unfavourably compared to pump-action combat shotguns. Likewise, there is little need to worry about internal movement disrupting aim at the moment of firing. That might be a factor on a long-range rifle shot, but with a short-range, deliberately imprecise weapon like a shotgun, a tiny movement in the aim point will not make any difference to your score.

Whatever kind of gun is chosen, the most important thing is that you are comfortable with it. Some lighter guns actually have more felt recoil than a heavy-barrelled 12-gauge, which can be unpleasant during a long session of shooting. Likewise, a certain amount of barrel weight aids in producing a steady swing; a lighter gun is more liable to jerk around and thus may be less accurate than expected.

As a starting choice, a decent all-round gun is probably best. It is wise to avoid over-specialized weapons, especially if you may also use your clay gun for shooting at the real thing from time to time. Overly long barrels are not a good choice, and it is generally better to stick with a middle-of-the-road design until you know for sure that you want something specific. The other advantage to buying a very mainstream gun is that it will be relatively easy to trade in against a new firearm if you decide to upgrade.

It may be worth considering getting a second-hand gun to start with, partly to reduce initial outlay and partly because new guns depreciate fast – just like cars. A good used gun can often be resold for only a little less than you originally paid for it, whereas a new gun will be resold at

Gun Etiquette Serves a Purpose

Most gun etiquette is ultimately about safety and the peace of mind of other shooters. For example, carrying a shotgun 'broken', i.e. with the barrels down and the chamber open and visibly empty, not only ensures that no accidents can occur, but also reassures others nearby that your weapon is in a safe condition.

The vast majority of gun-related accidents occur due to poor weapon handling. A gun that has no ammunition in the chamber cannot fire; keeping your weapon unloaded is the only way to absolutely prevent accidental discharges. However, you should always handle a gun as if it is loaded, even if you know it is not. Many accidents have occurred because the user 'knew' a weapon was unloaded and therefore felt it was safe to do something that would otherwise be rather foolish.

second-hand prices. It may be that you will love and cherish that first gun for the rest of your days, and you might expect to do so when you first decide to buy it, but you cannot be sure that you will not want to upgrade at some point, or to get rid of some of your expanding collection in return for permission to buy more guns.

Clay Pigeon Shooting Technique

Long ago, on a wet January day in Weardale, County Durham, I overheard a conversation behind the firing line. The gist of it was that one of the shooters had been asked what he did for recreation, and he had tried to explain. "So, you launch a clay pigeon up in the air and break it with a shotgun?" he was asked.

His wry answer was: "Well, most of the time we break the targets with the ground. But yes, we do fire a shotgun at some point." Self-deprecating humour aside, the fact is that everone misses at least some of the time. If you ever get to the point where you never miss, you've either discovered the outer limits of human capability or you're not challenging yourself enough.

The basic technique for hitting a small moving target with a shotgun is similar no matter whether it is made of clay or flesh and blood. The trick is to predict where the target is going to be and put a spread of shot around that point. Firing directly at the target

is pointless unless it is moving away from you or is attempting to fly down your gun barrel for some reason best known to itself.

It is possible to cheat if you know that the trap is set to a given trajectory and that the bird will be launched immediately you call for it. Knowing where the clay will be, and when, means you can simply aim at that point. Spot-shooting in this manner is a matter of timing on the call and trigger rather than actual shooting ability, and serves no purpose other than impressing gullible onlookers.

Firing Position

The process of hitting a target begins not when you take aim but when you move to your firing position. If your head is full of 'other stuff' – which might be anything from worrying about your tax return to trying to decide if you have the right choke in your gun – then your performance will suffer.

Preparation should be done – and done to your satisfaction – before you step up to the firing line. Even if you have maintained and adjusted your weapon to perfection, if you have doubts, then performance will again suffer. So do everything you need to before the shoot, and be sure you've done it. That way you can take up a shooting position both physically and mentally ready to shoot.

Mounting the gun (i.e. bringing it to your shoulder) is critically important.

Ear Protection

Ear protection can take the form of small plugs inserted in the ear, but some people do not like the sensation and prefer ear defenders, which are also easy to slip down around the neck when not in use.

Swing Through

The gun should be swung through the target and not brought immediately to a stop when the shot is taken. Instead, the swing continues in a smooth and natural manner.

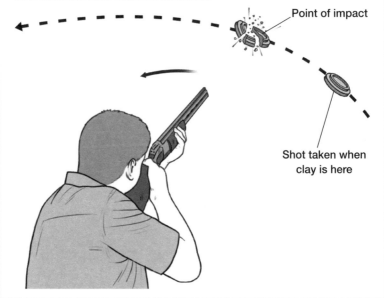

Point of impact

Shot taken when clay is here

Some competitions specify a gun-down starting position, i.e. it must be brought to the shoulder as part of taking the shot. Some shooters prefer to shoot this way even if it is not mandatory, not least because it is more realistic – wild birds are rarely obliging enough to appear at the precise moment your gun is ready, and there is a limit to how long you can stand in

firing position even if you happen to be aiming in the right direction.

In competitions where shooting is permitted from a gun-up starting position, the best scores tend to be made from this stance. It eliminates the delay in mounting the gun and thus gives more time to aim. However, the shooter is gaining information on the target and its trajectory while mounting his gun, so assuming the mount is smooth and efficient, the delay is not critical. A jerky or incompetent mount will likely result in a missed shot, however good the final marksmanship may otherwise be.

Even if you are in a gun-up position before calling for the clay, you still have to mount the gun correctly, but obviously you can make corrections before calling for a target. Fussing about for an extended period may infuriate other shooters and will generally wreck your aim anyway. So in the end you still need to mount your gun quickly and efficiently, and without the need for corrections.

The mechanism is to bring the gun to your eye line, not your head to the gun. The head must remain still during the mount to avoid disrupting the aim point. The stock is pulled into the 'shoulder pocket' between the shoulder joint and the collarbone so that the comb of the stock aligns with the side of the shooter's face. The gun need not be clutched in a death-grip, nor pulled in so hard that the shooter's body becomes tense – positive and firm is what is required.

There are various theories about where the muzzle(s) should point during all this activity. Some advocate a horizontal gun position, while some prefer a muzzle-up position. The muzzle should not come above the shooter's eye line in any case, and it should not wander about. The key to this is for both hands to work together, which requires practice. It is worth rehearsing mounting an empty gun many, many times for every shot actually taken.

The position of the firing hand is, of course, determined by the weapon's design, but there are many possible variations of supporting hand position. If the hand is too well forwards, then the gun may seem better controlled but the swing will be slower; conversely, a hand well to the rear allows a faster but poorly controlled swing. A comfortable, natural position allows for more instinctive handling of the weapon and reduces tension in the body, which may be worth more than a position advocated as 'perfect' but which does not suit a given shooter.

Often it is necessary to begin swinging to track a target before the mount is complete. Rushing the mount and then snatching a shot is not the route to success. Instead, it is necessary to pivot from the hips while the arms do their job of bringing the gun to the shoulder. These are separate but related actions, and if both are performed well, then the end result will be a mount that finishes up with the gun moving where it needs to go. Ideally, the body moves so that the eye can track the target, and the gun is brought up to join it.

Hitting the Target

With the gun mounted, all that remains is to shoot and hit the target – or to fire a shotgun into the

Browning Cynergy

The visually defining features of the Cynergy are its very pronounced top rib, ramped up at the back, angular woodwork, a shallow receiver profile and (in the Composite Sporting and Composite Field models) a fully adjustable stock. Cynergy Sporting models also have ported barrels, these venting off some of the firing gases to reduce muzzle flip, an advantage when a clay shooter needs to make a fast switch to the second of a pair. The futuristic look, however, is not just superficial. Indeed, the Cynergy is a totally new design for Browning, inside and out.

The extremely low receiver profile is the result of Browning's new MonoLock Hinge, which integrates the monobloc and the hinge as one and so avoids the need for trunnions and stub pins. Square-section pins are used for locking, and these, in a similar manner to Beretta's pin-locking, adjust themselves according to wear and tear.

Another internal revolution inside the Browning is the Reverse Striker ignition system. When the trigger is pulled, the coil springs travel backwards, striking rockers that then drive the firing pins forward. The effect is a crisp trigger pull and fast lock

time. Cartridge ejection is very brisk and, again unlike previous Brownings, the ejectors are set between the barrels rather than in the fore-end.

Cynergy shotguns are available in 12 or 20 gauges, and in barrel lengths ranging from 71cm (28in) to 81cm (32in). The barrels are also 'back-bored', meaning they are bored out to the maximum specifications for the cartridge, thereby alleviating friction on the shot as it travels down the barrel and reducing the number of pellet deformations (a principal cause of poor patterning).

Specifications: Browning Cynergy Sporting, Composite
Gauge/calibre: 12
Barrel length: 71cm (28in), 76cm (30in), 81cm (32in)
Weight: approx. 3.4kg (7.48lb)
Ejector type: automatic ejectors
Chokes: Invector-Plus interchangeable
Features: MonoLock Hinge; ported barrel; adjustable stock;
back-bored barrels

Mounting a Gun

Ready position

Bring to shoulder

sky and wait for the clay to fall to the ground, depending on your aim. Spot-shooting works well enough with clays, which follow a predictable trajectory. Using this technique you aim at a fixed point that the clay will reach – often late in its flight to allow it to slow down and begin to fall –

and shoot just before it gets there. This technique is not as useful for live targets, but for clays it does get good results. As noted, spot shooting is more about timing and judgement than accurate shooting. If you are going to shoot at the target rather than a point you hope it will occupy,

Mount position

There are various ways to mount a gun, but the key is to get it settled in the shoulder pocket without losing alignment with the target. Looking at the target the whole time, and bringing the gun onto the eye line, ensures a quick and efficient mount.

you need to lead the target. There are various ways to accomplish this.

Maintained Lead is a technique whereby the gun stays ahead of the target the whole time, essentially tracking a point ahead of the target. Different types of clay pigeon require

greater or lesser lead, as do faster/ slower and higher/lower targets, but judging the correct lead tends to become instinctive with practice.

Pull-Through (or swing-through) is almost the opposite of maintained lead. The gun starts behind the target and

Techniques Compared

Put simply, a swing-through starts behind the target and moves ahead, a pull-away starts on the target and pulls ahead, and a maintained lead starts ahead and stays ahead.

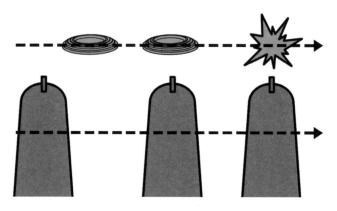

Swing-through

swings slightly faster than the target is moving. The aim point moves through the target, and when enough lead is obtained, the shot is taken. There may be a temptation to shoot when the aim point is on the target but this guarantees a miss behind.

Many experts believe that it is better to miss ahead of the target

by applying too much lead than to miss behind by applying too little – or in this case, none at all. A similar method to pull-through is to mount the gun with the aim point on the bird, or to begin the aiming process on the bird, and then move the aim point ahead until sufficient lead has been obtained.

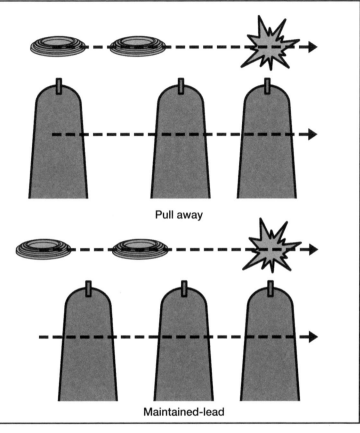

Pull away

Maintained-lead

Judging lead can only be learned from experience, but once you have mastered it, everything else is about making sure your shot goes where you want it. Overall, the key is to be ready before you shoot so that you don't have to sort out the contents of your mind and a bad body position while the bird is in the air, to mount the gun smoothly and well, and to swing in an unhurried and smooth motion – which might well still be fast. And, of course, not to get so excited or tense that you yank the trigger and undo the whole process. A wise man once commented that there is a magic pill you can take to perfect all of this, but it comes in a bottle marked 'time spent practising.'

The list of feathered prey for hunters is enormous, ranging from diminutive and solitary birds such as the snipe to great flocks of Canada geese, each weighing many kilos. The experience of hunting birds is equally varied, depending on your resources (often financial) and access to land. For some, a good day's bird hunting consists of little more than roaming woodland with an alert dog and a basic shotgun, hoping to spot and shoot anything that can be legally put on the table. For others with deep pockets, however, a day of driven pheasant shooting can cost hundreds, even thousands, of dollars if the shoot takes place on a prestigious estate.

Here we will look at the fundamentals of bird shooting, bearing in mind what has already been said about tracking and stalking. First, however, we need to take a deeper look into the world of shotgunning and the problems it can cause for the unwary.

The Art of Shotgunning

There are good reasons why a shotgun is used for bird shooting. While a rifle can be used against birds that are static on the ground, birds are most commonly shot on the wing, often when travelling at a considerable rate

....

A hunter, accompanied by his gun dog, shoots game from a cornfield.

6

Bird shooting is a very specific type of hunting, reliant principally on the use of a shotgun. Shotgunning is different to other types of shooting and requires many hours of practice.

Game Birds and Waterfowl

Field Hide

This is a basic hide used by a hunter for pigeon shooting. The hide needs to be comfortable for the shooter to spend several hours inside.

– some types of pigeon, for example, can fly at speeds of 100km/h (62mph). To hit a fast-moving bird with a single bullet would take legendary shooting ability. The shotgun, by contrast, can throw out a spread of shot that creates a pattern around the target, maximizing the chances of a hit on the bird even when in full flight.

The problem with shotgunning is that the weapon has been historically misrepresented in the media and films as a gun with which no one can miss a target. This idea couldn't be further from the truth. Shotguns typically have an effective range of 30–50m (98–164ft), so range alone is a limiting factor on whether you can hit some-

Shot Spread

With shotgunning, you are aiming to place the target bird in the centre of your shot spread, maximizing the number of impacts.

thing. As any field shooter knows, wild birds often have a seemingly uncanny ability to judge the range of a hunter's shotgun, staying just out of reach of all but the heaviest pellets. More importantly, even if a bird is within range the hunter only needs to be a centimetre or so out of alignment for the pattern of his shot to miss the prey entirely. Here, therefore, we need to address some of the core principles of effective shotgunning before we go on to study bird hunting proper.

Lead
When shooting moving targets like birds, especially if they are climbing, diving or flying across the field of

203

vision, the most critical factor in the effectiveness of the shot is lead. The word 'lead' quite simply refers to the allowance you have to make between the aimed point of the shot and the position of the bird (in this case) at the time you pull the trigger. In essence, you are shooting at the point where the bird will be by the time the shot reaches it; shooting directly at the bird will typically involve a miss behind, especially if the bird is crossing.

Understanding lead is essentially a process of experience, shooting at numerous targets and having an expert shot advise you on the correct lead, while also building up mental models of the correct 'lead picture' for each type of target. So, for example, you might find that when shooting a slow 'quartering' bird (crossing in front of you but travelling at an angle of around 45 degrees in relation to your position), the only lead you need is to shoot just in front of the bird's beak. If you are shooting a 'crosser' at altitude, however – such as a high-flying goose – you will need to shoot many feet in front of the target to achieve a hit. The permutations are many and subtle, and the best way to build up the lead pictures in your head is to shoot sporting clays (as opposed to skeet or trap) regularly, testing yourself on a wide variety of target presentations.

There are many schools of expert opinion on the best way to find the correct lead for your target, but three that warrant explanation are 'maintained lead', 'pull through' and 'point and push'. Note that in all these cases your should keep both your eyes open, as stereoscopic vision helps you to make more accurate lead and range adjustments.

Maintained lead

Maintained lead involves never letting your gun fall behind the bird. Keeping your eyes firmly on the target, you push the muzzles ahead of the bird as the gun comes to your shoulder, mounting the gun onto the lead point and pulling the trigger as soon as the stock is firmly in your shoulder and your cheek is down. (As a general rule, don't 'hang on to' a bird – constantly adjusting your aim and lead once the gun is in your shoulder. This process tends to result in your gun slowing down and shooting behind the target.)

Pull through

Here, you bring the muzzles of the gun up behind the bird, following the trajectory of its flight, then push the muzzles up and through the flight line, pulling the trigger as soon as the gun moves ahead of the target. (Another general rule – you need to keep the gun moving even as you pull the trigger; stopping the gun on the trigger pull is once again likely to result in a miss behind.) A good way to think of this technique is to imagine

Parallel Gun Mount

Mount the gun with the muzzles in line with the bird, keeping the barrels parallel.

Maintained Lead

When employing maintained lead, the hunter keeps his gun out ahead of the bird at all times, and keeps the barrel moving smoothly, even as he pulls the trigger.

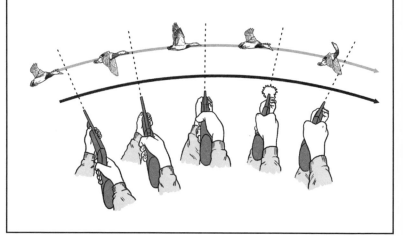

that the muzzle of the shotgun is a paintbrush, and you are painting a streak of colour through the bird's flight. British shooters also have a catchphrase to clarify the sweep of the gun across the target and the moment of firing: 'Butt, Belly, Beak, Bang.'

Point and push

In this technique, the gun is mounted directly onto the bird and follows it briefly in order to gain trajectory and speed information. Then the gun is

pushed ahead of the target and the trigger pulled.

Pros and Cons

The pros and cons of each technique are endlessly debated, and with some passion. However, the author maintains that all three have their utility depending on the target, and therefore you should get acquainted with the techniques on a clay ground to become a rounded shooter. Maintained lead, for example, is useful on crossing targets such as

Overhead Bird

This shooter is catching the pheasant as it climbs overhead. He swings up through the line of the bird's climb and pulls the trigger just as it disappears behind the muzzle.

geese where you have plenty of time to study before taking the shot. For a sudden bird that explodes from a bush just metres away from you in thick woodland, pull through might work best, as you could be forced by the terrain to swing your muzzles from behind. On a high incoming bird, such as a pheasant, point and push could give you the best way to make sense of the bird's flightline, especially as the bird will actually disappear behind your muzzles when you push the gun ahead to take the shot. Experiment constantly with the techniques until you find a mixture that works for you.

Birds and their Presentations

All birds have idiosyncratic flight patterns, and this is what makes bird hunting such a challenging pursuit. Woodcock, for example, can break suddenly from cover as your dog flushes it out, the bird adopting a fast jinking pattern of flight that challenges even the most competent shot. Duck, by contrast, can fly in swooping lines onto a pond, lake or river, the shooter waiting in his hide to bag a good specimen. The picture is complicated by the size and speed of the bird. For example, Canada geese can appear

Eye Dominance

If you are a right-handed shooter, you ideally want your right eye (i.e. the one that looks directly along the gun barrel) to be the dominant of the two eyes. To check this, point with your left index finger at a distant mark, keeping both your eyes open. Then close your left eye. If the index finger remains pointing at the target you are indeed right-eye dominant, but if it shifts off the mark, you could be either cross dominant or left-eye dominant. (Reverse the sides of the instructions above if you are a left-handed shooter.) Problems with dominance can explain many misses in shotgunning. Ways to compensate include (if you are right handed) partly closing your left eye the moment before your shoot, keeping your eyes glued firmly on the target (don't look at the barrel) and using your left index finger, extended up the fore-end of the gun, as a guide to your aiming point. (When using this last technique, think of shotgunning as accurate pointing rather than aimed shooting.)

Eye Dominance

The eyes should be focused where the barrels are pointing. Effective technique involves keeping the eyes locked on the target rather than looking at the barrel.

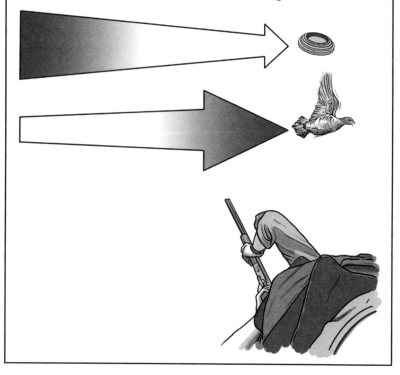

Clay versus High Bird

When shooting at high birds, the shooter should be aware that clays slow down in flight while game usually accelerates. For this reason, clay shooting is not necessarily good practice for bird shooting.

to be a relatively simple target when they fly overhead in a large skein. Yet their size often gives the illusion that they are flying slowly, resulting in the shooter giving them insufficient lead and missing the birds behind. Time in the field and some good book research will teach you about the ways that each type of bird flies, but it is useful to reflect on some general principles of how to handle distinctive patterns of flight.

Driven Birds

Driven birds refer to birds that fly in towards you, either directly or at an angle to your side, and from either in front or behind. Such birds can, quite literally, be driven onto your gun by beaters slashing their way through the undergrowth ahead, with pheasant being the classic driven game. The problem with driven birds is primarily one of body dynamics (yours, not the bird's). Most shotgunning is conducted with the body's weight squarely on the front foot, pushing the shoulders forwards and into the gun. With driven birds, the presentation can force the cheek to lift off the stock as the shooter arches his body upwards, resulting in inaccurate shooting.

If the bird is flying from your front to back, mount the gun with the weight still on the front foot and maintain this posture until the muzzles are nearing the vertical. If you haven't taken the shot by now, lift up the heel of the front foot and allow your body weight to transfer smoothly to the back leg, which allows you to swing your gun through the perpendicular. When a bird is flying from the opposite direction (from behind you) start with your weight on the back leg, your head raised to the sky to spot the target. Once you have seen the bird, begin to mount the gun while shifting the weight back onto the front leg.

Crossing Shots

Crossing birds are those that fly directly, or at an angle, across your frontal field of vision. They can be infuriating shots to take, not least because the smallest error in lead will result in a miss either in front or behind, while a misjudgement in the bird's trajectory will put the shot above or below. Crossing birds are often suited to a maintained lead approach. As soon as you see the bird, lock your eyes onto it and quickly 'see' the correct lead picture in front of the bird. (If it helps, imagine a shadow projecting from the front of the bird's beak, the tip of the shadow being the correct lead distance.) Mount the gun quickly and smoothly and shoot once it is in your shoulder. You won't have time to judge the lead picture meticulously, but neither should you rush the shot.

All shotgun shooting should be a smooth, flowing process from raising the gun to pulling the trigger, with no awkward time lags or gaps at any stage. Note that with crossing birds (or indeed any presentation of bird) that are flying lower than your shooting position, such as down in the bottom of a valley, ensure that all your weight is sunk heavily down

Types of Bird

Game birds come in a wide variety of shapes and sizes. This can range from large geese to small ducks, the former requiring shotguns firing heavy loads of shot.

over your front foot and that your cheek is squarely on the upper part of the stock.

Going Away Birds

Birds that fly directly away from you can be among the easiest to shoot. If they fly straight and low, all you really need to do is shoot straight at them. As long as it is in range and your gun is properly mounted, you should hit the target. If you don't, it is likely that you have misread some of the subtle elements in the flight pattern. The backdrop a bird flies against, for example, can often confuse the eye, especially if the horizon or a ridgeline follows a slightly different alignment to the bird's trajectory.

If the bird is quartering, i.e. flying away at an angle to you, you will have to lead the bird off to the side it is travelling towards. The amount of lead you have to apply obviously depends upon the angle at which it is flying in relation to you, but as a general rule, avoid extreme amounts of lead except when the angle means that the bird is virtually a crosser. More important is to spot where you want to kill the bird from the moment you start mounting the gun, and con-centrate all your efforts on that point.

Incoming Birds

Handling an incoming bird, especially one that is dropping rapidly, has special relevance for the wildfowler who has to tackle ducks and geese

Shooting from a Lying Position

Shooting from your back can be tricky, as the ground can interfere with the free movement of your arms and gun. However, it may improve concealment and give more opportunities for a shot.

coming in to land at a pond or body of water. The incoming bird under these circumstances can be losing

speed and height at the same time, so judging the correct lead beneath it is awkward. The point and push

beneath and pull the trigger. If the bird is flying towards you, don't feel that you have to let it reach too close before taking the shot. As the distance between you and bird closes, so your shot string tightens – leaving a bit of distance can improve your chances of a hit.

Hunting Techniques

The most basic method of bird hunting, particularly for species such as quail, pheasant, grouse, chukar and partridge, is simply to go walking through woodland or thick vegetation with a well-trained dog and your gun at the ready. The dog can be of either the flushing or pointing type, and the working dynamic between dog and owner must be smooth and dependable.

In areas where game are scattered over large distances, it is not unusual to find flushing done by quad bikes and similar off-road vehicles, with the shooters ready to fire directly from the vehicle. One important safety note here – take great care when travelling in vehicles with loaded guns. Trigger mechanisms can be sensitive to abrupt knocks, so at all times ensure that the barrel of the gun is pointed away from the vehicle and its occupants, and kept fully under control.

can be a good technique on these birds – keep the muzzles on the target to gauge its movement, then drop

As always, you should research your bird types thoroughly before heading off on a shoot. Note, for

Falco SO27A

Falco makes .410s in both single- and double-barrelled versions, the latter including the SO27A. The SO27A is an over-and-under weapon fitted with 70cm (27.5in) barrels. These are choked at Modified and Full, the tight chokes being essential for making decent killing patterns at distance from the small loads of the .410 cartridges. Chambers are set for 76mm (3in) magnum cartridges, and using the SO27A with no.6 shot makes the gun suitable for a range of vermin and game, such as rabbits, rats, crows and squirrels, depending on the range and the shot presentation.

In terms of operating features, the SO27A has double triggers and the safety switch is manual. Automatic safety switches tend to be more common on field guns, so extra care is needed when using the SO27A in company. As with most .410s, the SO27A is a light weapon, weighing only 2.7kg (6lb).

For those wanting a side-by-side .410 gun, Falco's basic SO27 model fills the gap. In many ways specifications are the same

as the SO27A, although the slimmer side-by-side configuration trims another 0.2kg (0.5lb) off the overall weight. Guns available in the .410 calibre are currently going through something of a renaissance. The small calibre is ideal for use in light hunting roles, such as vermin control. Falco not only make .410 guns with a conventional shotgun layout, but also a series with true pistol grips (no shoulder stocks) with either external hammers or a hammerless arrangement.

Specifications: Falco SO27A
Gauge/calibre: .410
Barrel length: 70cm (27.5in)
Weight: 2.7kg (6lb)
Ejector type: extractors
Chokes: fixed

Shooting Party

There is an etiquette to shooting in a group. Nobody likes it when someone else bags the bird they were about to take, so a measure of restraint is advisable.

Common North American Quail Types for Hunting

Bobwhite quail tend to inhabit uncultivated land, especially ditches, hedgerows, brush and some pinewoods. Best hunting times are mid morning and afternoon, and after rain.

California quail live in brushy open areas and uncultivated farmland, eating seeds, grain, fruit and berries. Covey scatters into undergrowth when startled and remains hidden until older birds signal 'all clear'.

Mountain quail are large quail often found around steep, grassy hillsides, eating oats, grain and rye. Flush the birds by moving down the hillside, not up (in the latter case, they will simply run uphill through the brush).

Scaled quail live in arid, brushy terrain near water holes and ponds. When startled they can run at 25km/h (15mph), so will often be shot on the ground.

example, that there can be distinct differences in the behaviours and physical characteristics of sub-species. The ruffed grouse of North America likes to inhabit thick foliage and brush on the edge of young forests or forest openings, feeding on berries, fruit and grasses. It is a fast-flying bird, apt to leap from cover when startled and whiz off out of sight among trees. The sage grouse, by contrast, spends its life around the sagebrush plant, growing stout in the process and consequently being a rather sluggish flier as well as a tasty meal. The moral is, don't assume a one-size-fits-all approach to hunting.

Decoying

Another popular method of bird hunting is that of decoying. This involves luring birds into a feeding area with either bird models or using dead birds, propped up with sticks or wire to give a living appearance. Pigeon hunting is a good case in point. Woodpigeons tend to live in specific areas of woodland situated conveniently between the agricultural fields (especially those that have been

Pigeon Hunting

The hunter has positioned an arc of pigeon decoys to the maximum range of his shotgun, the shooting hide facing directly into the flightline.

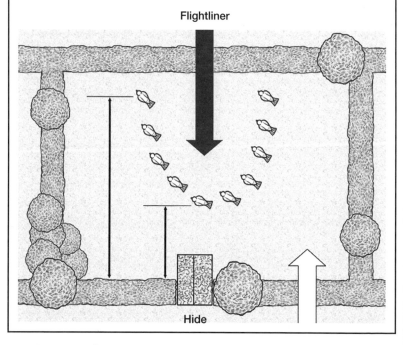

Flightliner

Hide

recently harvested) in which they like to feed. The routes between the woods and the fields are known as flightlines, and they act as predictable routes for the birds to follow. If you are intending to hunt pigeon in an area, always do a recce trip first, observing the flightlines that the birds take and

all the stop-off points along the way (trees, fences, telegraph wires, etc). The route will often follow the line of the prevailing wind.

The next step in the process is to set out your decoy pigeons. These can be bought from good hunting suppliers, and their level of sophistication is extremely variable. Some are nothing more than plastic pigeon silhouettes, while others are realistically proportioned 3D models that are fixed on bobbing pieces of wire to simulate an active bird. At the top of the range there are electrically animated models that appear to flap and feed to an unsuspecting real-life pigeon. The essential point about the decoy is that it attracts the birds to the field and gives them a sense that all is well.

To capitalize on the pigeons' flight paths, and the lure of the decoys, you should build a well-camouflaged hide that gives you clear shooting across or into their flightline. The hide needs to be well constructed, concealing you effectively from your prey while also allowing you free movement of the gun. Once you are in place – later afternoon is often the best time for hunting pigeon – then, hopefully, the birds will fly straight to your gun along the flightline. Those people who have become expert in such methods of pigeon shooting can achieve very large bags in a single day, up to several dozen birds.

Wildfowling

Wildfowling is another form of bird shooting that benefits from decoying. Goose decoys can be placed in a field where geese like to feed, the hunter then establishing himself in a hide or blind overlooking the field to await dawn or dusk. Duck decoys – about a dozen is a good number

People Can Be Unlucky or Just Plain Dumb

It is not safe to assume that the people around you will not do something unsafe, irresponsible or downright stupid. Someone could blunder into you from behind, and there have been incidents of people blithely walking in front of the firing line. Usually this is due to preoccupation with a task or because the bystanders are unaware of the shooter, but the reason does not matter. It is necessary to assume that anyone around you could possibly endanger themselves. Stand clear of anyone who might accidentally jostle you, and watch downrange for people who might somehow appear in your line of fire at the worst possible moment. It's rare but it happens.

U.S. Fish and Wildlife Service – approved shot types for wildfowling

Approved shot type*	Percent composition by weight	Field testing device**
Bismuth-tin	97 bismuth, and 3 tin	Hot Shot7***
Iron (steel)	Iron and carbon	Magnet or Hot Shot7
Iron-tungsten	Any proportion of tungsten, and >1 iron	Magnet or Hot Shot7
Iron-tungsten-nickel	>1 iron, any proportion of tungsten and up to 40 nickel	Magnet or Hot Shot7
Tungsten-bronze	51.1 tungsten, 44.4 copper, 3.9 tin and 0.6 iron, or 60 tungsten, 35.1 copper, 3.9 tin and 1 iron	Rare earth magnet
Tungsten-iron-copper-nickel	40-76 tungsten, 10-37 iron, 9-16 copper and 5-7 nickel	Hot Shot7 or rare earth magnet
Tungsten-matrix	95.9 tungsten, 4.1 polymer	Hot Shot7
Tungsten-polymer	95.5 tungsten, 4.5 nylon 6 or 11	Hot Shot7
Tungsten-tin-iron	Any proportions of tungsten and tin, and >1 iron	Magnet or Hot Shot7
Tungsten-tin-bismuth	Any proportions of tungsten, tin and bismuth	Rare earth magnet
Tungsten-tin-iron-nickel	65 tungsten, 21.8 tin, 10.4 iron and 2.8 nickel	Magnet
Tungsten-iron-polymer	41.5-95.2 tungsten, 1.5-52.0 iron and 3.5-8.0 fluoropolymer	Magnet or Hot Shot7

* Coatings of copper, nickel, tin, zinc, zinc chloride and zinc chrome on approved nontoxic shot types also are approved.

** This column is for information only, it is not regulatory.

*** The Hot Shot field-testing device is from Stream Systems of Concord, CA.

Taking High Shots

Normally, the shooter would lean into the gun, but when taking a high shot, it is necessary to drop onto the back foot instead. There is a limit to how high an angle you can take and remain stable.

Using a Gun Dog

A gun dog is a valuable hunting aid, but has to be well trained. A dog that gets frightened or overexcited is, at best, an embarrassment and may cause a hazard to itself or others.

Ruger Red Label

Like many successful shotguns, Ruger's Red Label is available in a range of calibres, notably 20 gauge and 12 gauge. A 28-gauge version is available for those who want a lighter gun with less recoil.

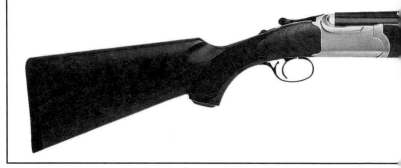

– can be sited on and around a lake or pond. (There are even advanced duck decoy models today that not only paddle around a pond, but also dip their heads under the water and make authentic quacking sounds.) Remember that you are now in a specific wildfowl environment, and a blind that would look perfectly at home in brushland might stick out like a sore thumb amid the reeds and grasses bordering a lake. Whatever you do, make sure that your blind or hide utilizes local foliage as camouflage, or at least patterned man-made camouflage.

Your problems intensify when constructing a wildfowling blind if there is a paucity of cover available, such as occurs in an open field where large flocks of geese come to feed. In these situations, you may have to dig a purpose-built pit in the earth, which you then camouflage with overhead cover to disguise your presence from the air. This process could well take some effort on your part, and you will probably have to do it the day before you go out on the hunt. Select a spot with good drainage, however, or you could come back in the pre-dawn darkness to find that your hideout has filled with water overnight.

Ensure that if you do go wild-fowling, you take with you appropriate shot. In many countries the use of

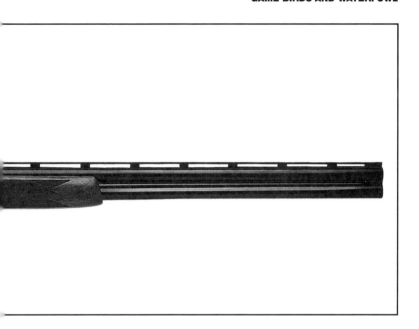

lead shot for wildfowling is prohibited. This is on account of the fact that the lead pellets used by wildfowlers often end up being ingested by ducks, who naturally eat dirt and grit to aid their digestive processes. Ducks have then been observed to develop lead poisoning, often with fatal or certainly distressing results.

Some hunting organizations have contested the results of the studies, but the balance of scientific evidence seems to be overwhelmingly stacked against them. Therefore, it is our responsibility, as responsible hunters, to comply with the findings and use some of the many nontoxic forms of shot now available (see table). When

the early non-toxic varieties became mandatory, there was much despair among wildfowlers. Not only were the new cartridges expensive, the steel and tungsten/iron shot inside them was much harder but lighter than lead. This meant that not only was the shot unsuitable for many shotgun barrels and chokes, but the shot had less range (its lightness meant that it slowed down faster in the air) and imparted less kinetic energy to the target.

For some wildfowlers, this led to them either giving up their hunting pastime or advocating non-compliance and running the risk of legal action – not to mention adding to the lead problem in the

Bring the Right Gun!

There is a persistent but probably apocryphal tale of a foreign dignitary who turned up at a shoot on the Scottish moors armed with a submachinegun. Although probably less effective than a shotgun for the purpose at hand, this weapon was inappropriate for all kinds of other reasons, and the appropriateness of a weapon must be considered as a social as well as a practical matter.

environment. Thankfully, science has marched on and there are now advanced nontoxic shot types that provide lead-like performance and which can be used with any chokes in a shotgun. When you go out wildfowling, however, ensure that you clear out any lead cartridges from your pockets, so you don't load the old type by mistake. If you are pass shooting – shooting at geese

Many game birds have very good eyesight, which makes camouflage of the hunter and weapon extremely important.

Turkey Call

Turkey call devices can be used to attract a turkey to a hunter's position. The lid is scraped across the box to produce a range of squawks.

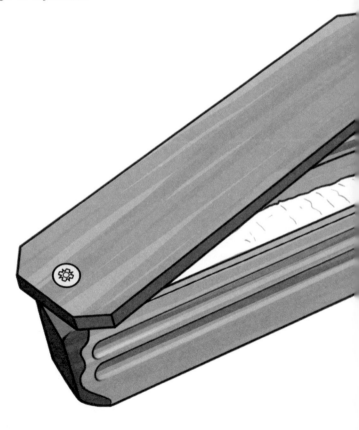

flying high overhead on the way to feeding grounds – ensure that you have heavy cartridge loads and a gun with full choke to give you the reach and penetration required. Geese feathers can be surprisingly resistant to shot, so you need to ensure that you have the right cartridges and gun configuration to punch through.

Turkey Shooting

Wild turkeys are worlds apart from the creatures that tend to end up on people's plates over Thanksgiving and Christmas. They have excellent eyesight, great camouflage in woodland environments and can fly, so getting close to a wild turkey, never mind shooting one, can present a considerable challenge. They are also large creatures – an adult male (known as a 'gobbler' or 'tom') can weigh up to 11kg (24lb) – so you need a fully choked shotgun firing a heavy grade of shot to bring one down convincingly.

You should start your turkey shooting by first carefully patrolling a known turkey area without a gun, armed only with a turkey call device. The turkey call imitates the various sounds made by a hen to attract a gobbler. To perform these calls convincingly takes some practice and knowledge, and if done improperly or excessively, they are liable to make the gobbler go quiet and move away from the area. A response from the gobbler, however,

Full Camouflage

This hunter is dressed in full camouflage, including a face mask – wild turkeys can be spooked by a flash of bare skin. The hunter is also using a cross-pole support to steady his gun.

will confirm that wild turkeys are indeed in the area, and droppings, feathers and tracks (usually found in muddy river banks) will provide further evidence. You now have the information you need to return for the hunt. When you do go back, top to bottom camouflage is a must.

Ensure that every scrap of skin is concealed, as the perceptive turkey will doubtless spot you and flee into the woods where you are unlikely to find it again.

Have your gun loaded and at the ready. Note that many turkey shooters also buy shotguns that

are themselves covered with camouflage patterning.

For the hunt itself, use the call to attract a gobbler and then find a vantage spot such as a broad tree, the dimensions of which are wider than your torso. Sit with the tree behind you to disperse your visual outline, and allow the turkey to approach within about 35m (115ft). You target area is the turkey's head and neck. Note that when a turkey is strutting around, its neck is contracted, presenting an even smaller target. Wait until the turkey has finally stopped strutting and extends its neck, then take the shot.

Savage Model 210FT Turkey Gun

The Savage Model 210FT Turkey Gun has one hunting purpose, and press reviews of the gun in action acknowledge it as a capable turkey killer within the range of its 76mm (3in) shells.

Bolt-action shotguns are not common weapons, and by far the majority of turkey-hunting guns are semi-auto shotguns or break-action guns. However, the Savage Turkey Gun is well designed for its purpose. Like its slug gun counterpart, it has a 61cm (24in) barrel, the difference in this case being the interchangeable choke tube. Only one choke tube is supplied with the gun – a tightly bored choke suitable for turkey shooting – but the 210FT will also take standard choke tubes from several other makes of 12-gauge shotgun.

As turkey hunting involves aimed rather than instinctively pointed shots, the 210FT has open sights as standard. The sights are very simple – a rear V-notch corresponding with a simple brass bead front sight. These sights may in themselves be sufficient for turkey shooting, as the range of a standard 76mm (3in) 12-gauge shell is only around 30–40m (98–131ft). However, turkey shooting also requires some precision to target the right part of the bird or spot

it among the foliage in the first place. The 210FT receiver is also drilled and tapped for a scope mount, and the 60-degree of rotation means that operating the bolt handle stays well clear of a scope.

To handle its 12-gauge loads, the 210FT has a very substantial bolt action, the bolt alone weighing just under 0.7kg (1.5lb). The bolt head rotates to lock before firing, and dual extractors and a powerful ejection spring ensure positive removal of the spent cartridges. The Turkey Gun is fed from a two-shell-capacity box magazine. The stock of the 210FT is fitted with a recoil pad and the standard colour scheme is camouflage.

Specifications: Savage Model 210FT Turkey Gun
Calibre: 12-gauge
Barrel length: 61cm (24in)
Weight: 3.4kg (7.5lb)
Sights: open; drilled and tapped for scope mounts
Mechanism: bolt action, magazine fed

Making the shot is only part of the skill of hunting. Long before you bring down a quarry, you must put yourself in a position where you can make the attempt. Some hunting expeditions fail right from the outset, going out looking for game that isn't there due to lack of knowledge of terrain or the habits of the quarry. Taking the wrong equipment, lacking the right camouflage or hides, or having to abort the trip due to bad weather can all cause hunters to come home without even sighting their quarry.

A certain level of respect for the prey is necessary for successful hunting. Animals are skilled at staying alive in their own environment, despite the attentions of humans and other predators. To a creature that has lived in the woods all of its life, the human city-dweller who thinks he is being clever and stealthy may in fact be extremely obvious. Thus it is necessary to have patience rather than blundering about the boonies, gun in hand, in the hope of encountering nature's most stupid animals. You might get lucky, but it is not likely.

Hunting can be dangerous in various ways. Weather and hazards

• •

Some hunters like to carry combination guns, usually with one shotgun and one rifle barrel. This allows a degree of flexibility not available with a single gun, but at the price of extra weight.

7

The most important part of hunting is preparation. Getting into the right area with the correct camouflage and a suitable gun allows a chance at a successful shot.

Hunting Game

Using Cover

A hunter whose camouflage is generally the same colour as vegetation behind him will be hard for game to spot, but one who skylines himself may stand out. Be aware of your backdrop.

like hidden gulleys, thorny bushes and swampy areas can bring a trip to an unpleasant end, and of course many animals can be dangerous. Most game will flee when startled or shot at, but some 'prey' creatures are prone to turn on a threat, especially if protecting young.

It is important not to focus too closely on what you are hunting; at least not to the exclusion of other creatures. A given animal will not understand that it is not your intended prey, and may attack to defend territory or young, even though you know you are not a threat to it. Similarly, an animal you discounted because you were not stalking it will still flee if it detects you, which might warn your intended quarry of your presence.

It is also unwise to discount the possibility of other humans posing a threat, either indirectly by disturbing the local wildlife and/or triggering an attack by a territorial creature, or more directly by irresponsible shooting. There is a popular comedy song about a hunter who bagged 'two game wardens, seven hunters and a cow' by a simple method: 'you just stand there looking cute, and when something moves... you shoot.'

Most hunters are rather more responsible than that, but the fact remains that some people can become a little trigger-happy out in the wilds, especially if they think there is no one else around. You cannot guarantee

Small and Big Targets

A very powerful gun is not desirable when shooting small game, unless the aim is to vaporize the target. A light gun is inhumane for larger targets, however, as it will wound rather than killi.

that there is not someone out there who will shoot at movements or the merest flash of something vaguely the right colour seen through the undergrowth. One common safety tip is not to wear anything coloured white or tan during deer-hunting season, and to use high-visibility clothing such

as hunter orange, and making other hunters aware of your presence is wise. If you hunt with a dog, it should also have a high-visibility vest.

Hunting Methods

Small game is best hunted with a fairly light weapon – there is no

point in blasting your dinner to pieces – and using an opportunistic approach. Moving slowly and quietly, you should be able to spot numerous animals such as rabbit or squirrel. These small, agile creatures are not an easy target once they take off running or zip around the trunk of a tree, so you must be prepared to take whatever shots you are offered.

In order to be able to bring down enough small game to be worth eating, you need to be able to spot targets and make a quick shoot/no-shoot decision depending mainly on whether the shot is safe to take but

Mountain Landscape

It is important to know the terrain you intend to hunt over – how the colours blend and the shadows fall. The animals that live there will spot anything that looks out of place, like a clueless hunter wearing the wrong camouflage.

also on the chance of actually hitting the target. If the animal can be shot before it starts to move, your chances are much better than trying to hit a zig-zagging hare going at full speed across rough ground. However, with skill, such a shot can be made, especially if you can predict where the animal might head for and prepare the shot a little.

Some animals will instinctively seek places that would grant safety from natural predators, but which offer no protection against a gun. A creature that runs up a tree and then sits still might expect to be safe from most predators, but it will actually make itself an easier target for the hunter. Understanding the habits of the prey can grant opportunities to make relatively easy shots.

One danger with any sort of fast-moving animal is that it might go out of sight, and you cannot guarantee that it is safe to shoot into that bush or clump of grass. A willingness to abort the shot is necessary for safe hunting, frustrating though that may be. However, a fleeing creature that enters, for example, an area of bushes, may well come out again at a predictable point. It is sometimes possible to track a fleeing quarry, even though you can't see it, based on your perception of its speed and direction. Once it re-emerges and you can see that it is safe to shoot, you may already have your shot set up.

Beretta SSO6

The Beretta SSO6 utilizes Beretta's SO shotgun action to produce a heavy-duty break-action over-and-under rifle, and demonstrates how breech-loading guns are well suited to the most powerful rifled rounds. The SSO6 is derived from the action of the SO shotguns, and indeed the SSO6 can take a set of shotgun barrels to give the shooter true versatility on a long hunting trip. Typical of many double-barrelled rifles, the SSO6 is designed to fire large-calibre, heavy-charge shells during big-game hunting.

The rifle calibres are .458 Winchester Mag., .375 H&H Mag. and the 9.3x74R. These are all venerable big-game calibres (the .375 H&H Mag., for example, was developed in 1912) and the recoil generated on firing the 270- or 300-grain bullet is extremely heavy. The .458 round is even heavier at around 500 grains, and both will stop the largest of land animals. The 9.3x74R is not quite as forceful as the other calibres, and has less muzzle energy (hence it is often found in light double guns), so is not used for the largest game animals, but it is still a powerful round for hoofed creatures. A trapdoor for additional cartridges is fitted in the stock.

The SSO6's rifled barrel is 61cm (24in), and comes with a simple blade front sight and a corresponding V-notch rear sight. However, an optical Zeiss scope can also be fitted, the sight attaching to the top barrel via claw mounts.

The sight is set out to 100m (328ft), and the relatively short range is practical, as the movement of breaking open and closing the barrels can cause more disruption to the sight than on a fixed-barrel gun, although the gun will be accurate well beyond this range.

Specifications: Beretta SSO6
Gauge/calibre: 12/.458 Winchester Mag, .375 H&H Mag, 9.3x74R
Barrel length: 61cm (24in), 76cm (28in)
Weight: 5kg (11lb)
Ejector type: automatic ejectors
Chokes: interchangeable, fixed or rifled barrels

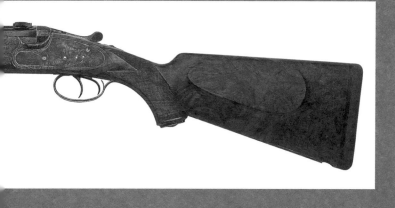

Larger game such as deer require a different approach and also a relatively powerful rifle, partly to ensure that a large animal can be brought down with a single shot and partly because the shot must often be taken at a greater distance. Deer, in particular, are extremely perceptive of threats and will flee readily. As with any prey animal, it is worth understanding the habits of the creature and the terrain it lives in, both in general terms and also specifically the area in which you intend to hunt.

An expedition to observe the area where you intend to hunt – perhaps undertaken before the season begins – can pay dividends. You may be able to determine good spots to hide, avenues of approach to places where deer are likely to be and other positive information, and also learn about the region's characteristics so that you can avoid making mistakes when the actual hunt begins.

Stalking

Deer and similar large game can be hunted by stalking, although this requires excellent woodcraft skills and a great deal of patience. It is necessary to remain downwind of the quarry, which dictates the opportunities you will have for concealment. What looks like a good avenue of approach may not be one if the wind shifts and gives you away, so knowledge of local conditions is essential. It will probably take a long time to get into position to shoot, and any urge to hurry must be curbed or you will waste all the effort invested to get to that point.

Hides

Alternatively, you can take up position in a hide and wait for game to enter the area. This requires a lot of patience; staring at the same patch of windswept moorland for hours on end is a definition of 'fun' that few people would subscribe to. Observation of the animals' habits will give a good indication of when and where they will be, but there are never any guarantees. It is necessary to be stealthy about entering and leaving your hide, and of course while observing you will not be able to move around much.

A hide should be carefully examined to see it is safe to use before entering. There are relatively few possible hazards if the hide is at ground level, but high seats, platforms or hides constructed in the trees can become unsafe over time – and not all are constructed to very high standards in the first place.

Another option is to use the natural skittishness of prey animals against them, driving one or more animals towards a waiting shooter by producing noise or movement in a different direction. Again, observation of the ground ahead of time will help determine a good position

Camouflage Tent Hide

A tent hide offers good concealment as well as some protection from inclement weather. However, it cannot be tailored to different environments and must still be sited well to avoid standing out.

for the shooters. Ideally the quarry should be channelled into a narrow area, curtailed by terrain, allowing the shot to be prepared ahead of time. With smaller game, it is relatively easy to put the animal down with a single shot, but larger quarry like deer require more precision.

A shot to the heart/lung area or one that strikes the spine will drop

High Seat

Whilst rather exposed to the elements, a high seat offers a good field of view and a vantage point above the level of vegetation and many ground features.

even a large deer very quickly, but most other hits will not. A quick kill is desirable not only for humane reasons but also to prevent the injured animal from running off and possibly alarming everything else in the region.

Even a dying animal can run a surprisingly long way, and may clear obstacles that might otherwise seem impossible. Even one that goes down

Oregon Department of Fish and Wildlife – firearms hunting safety tips

The four primary rules of firearm safety:

MUZZLE Control the direction of your muzzle at all times.

TRIGGER Keep your finger outside of the trigger guard until ready to shoot.

ACTION Treat every firearm as though it were loaded – open the action and visually check if it is loaded. Firearms should be unloaded with actions open when not actually in use.

TARGET Be sure of your target and what is in front of it and beyond it.

The most common causes of hunting incidents are:

- Hunter judgment mistakes, such as mistaking another person for game or not checking the foreground or background before firing.
- Safety rule violations, including pointing the muzzle in an unsafe direction and ignoring proper procedures for crossing a fence, obstacle or difficult terrain.

Other causes of hunting incidents:

- Lack of control and practice, which can lead to accidental discharges and stray shots.
- Mechanical failure, such as an obstructed barrel, improper ammunition or malfunctioning safety.

– www.dfw.state.or.us/resources/hunting/safety/index.asp

Sako Quad Hunting Rifle

Like many small-game rifles, the Sako Quad can be chambered for various calibres of ammunition. Barrels and magazines are constructed so that those set up for differing calibres will not fit together.

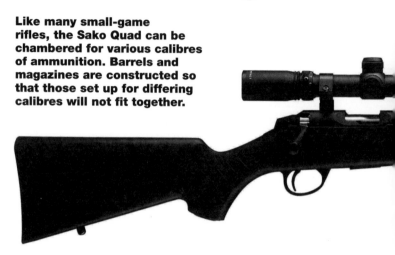

quickly might disappear from sight and require tracking. It is unwise to immediately rush to check a kill; an apparently dead animal might lurch back into life and try to escape at your approach, whereas if there is no immediate threat in the vicinity it is more likely to stay put until it is too weak to move anyway.

After a few minutes you will need to approach the quarry and check that it really is dead. If not, the animal should be dispatched cleanly, usually by a shot to the spine in the neck region. You may have to track a wounded quarry for some distance, but even if you did not intend to eat it there is a

certain moral responsibility to end the suffering of anything you have shot. A blood trail is usually sufficient to lead you to a kill, but a large, wounded animal fleeing in a panic is unlikely to be very subtle so there may be a trail smashed through undergrowth and low branches to make the direction even more obvious.

Hunting dangerous animals such as bear or boar is not something to be undertaken lightly, not least because these creatures may not be stopped by a rifle bullet. Hunters operating in areas where these animals live should be constantly aware of the possibility of an encounter, even

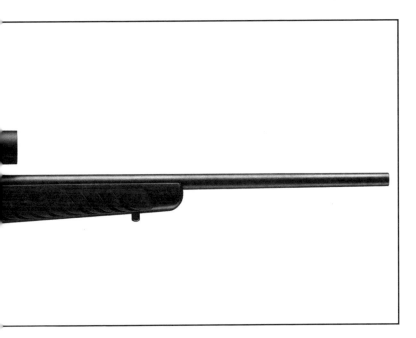

if they are hunting something entirely different.

A large-calibre weapon is necessary for any dangerous creature, and even then this does not guarantee a quick kill. For that reason semi-automatics are sometimes favoured, and it is wise to hunt in a team. Even if the target is hit and apparently downed, you should remain wary and ready to shoot again – do not immediately approach the target. There may be other threats in the area even if your target really is unable to strike back.

As with any form of shooting sport, it is wise to check on local regulations before setting off. Laws on what

targets can be shot where – and with what guns – can be complex, and a trip that brings home some game plus a big fine may not, on balance, turn out to have been much of a success.

Hunting Equipment

Aside from outdoor clothing and camping gear, the two main items needed for hunting are guns and vision aids. Many guns come with or can be fitted with a telescopic sight, which is essential for clean shooting at longer distances. The sight can also be used to search for a target, but this is not ideal. Binoculars or a spotting scope are more generally

Consider the Backstop

It is important to consider what is behind the target before shooting. Ideally, a hillside forms an excellent backstop, or if hunting you may be shooting somewhat downwards, in which case you can be sure that the bullet will go into the ground somewhere safe. When shooting at birds in the air, a clear area behind the target ensures that shot falling back to earth does not endanger anyone.

Spotting Scope

A spotting scope can be used by a spotter helping a shooter find game, or by the hunter himself. It is much easier to raise a small scope to the eye than to level a rifle every time the hunter wants to look at something in the distance.

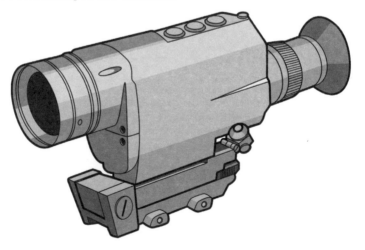

useful for searching and observing than a scope, not least because they are easy to carry and deploy. You are less likely to be spotted taking out a small spotting scope or a pair of binoculars than raising a rifle to look through the sights, and the field of view is also wider. A separate vision aid for searching allows you to leave the rifle on its sling or in its case, and to search more quickly with less effort than with your rifle sights.

Other vision equipment may sometimes be useful, such as a lamp/scope combination or low-light equipment. These items make hunting at night easier, although they can be heavy and expensive. Their applications are somewhat specialized, and for most hunting trips they are simply not necessary.

Although many people associate hunting with telescopic sights, there are many applications where traditional iron sights are actually more useful. When shooting at long range there is no substitute for a good scope, but at shorter distances it is quicker to acquire the target using iron sights. A telescopic sight is probably unnecessary at close range and may impose enough delay in aiming that a fleeting target is lost.

It is not possible to determine a 'best overall gun for hunting' because the applications vary so much. When selecting a gun, it is important to consider not just the expected target but also the likely terrain that will

be shot over, and of course your own preferences.

A semi-automatic weapon is an entirely viable option, although under most circumstances the ability to make a second shot very quickly will not be used. It might, however, be useful in a 'target-rich environment', allowing a quick shot at a second quarry flushed by the first shot, and could perhaps be a lifesaver if attacked by a dangerous animal such as a bear. Semi-automatic weapons are often strictly controlled; although legal in many areas, they may be prohibited from hunting by local legislation.

Most hunting rifles are mechanical repeaters, using the manual operation of the mechanism (usually a bolt or lever action) to reload. Weapons of this sort are well suited to making the kind of precise, single shots necessary for successful hunting. As a very general rule, lever-action weapons tend to be shorter than bolt-action rifles, which can be useful in close terrain or where the rifle has to be brought around quickly to tackle a suddenly appearing target.

Calibre is a difficult question. There are many opinions about the ideal calibre for any given prey. For small animals and vermin, a small-calibre rimfire cartridge is fine. Their relatively low power minimizes recoil and also reduces the danger from ricochets and missed shots. More powerful cartridges may kill at long distances – this is after all what they are designed

Vantage Point

It is worth stopping to have a good look around from time to time, getting a feel for the terrain and its subtler features. A good vantage point is also useful when searching for signs of game, such as tracks and paths, and of course for the game themselves.

to do – but a small-calibre gun has a much smaller danger space.

For larger prey such as deer, powerful centre-fire cartridges are necessary. Opinions vary as to the optimum calibre but .30-06 (or 7.62x51mm) is a good all-round starting point. Larger calibres are generally only used for dangerous prey and are the territory of the experienced and specialist hunter. Similarly, combination weapons are not normally a good choice for beginning hunters. A combination rifle/shotgun or a rifle with barrels of different calibres does offer additional options for unexpected targets, but for most purposes it is not worth carrying the extra weight.

Tracking

Successful trapping skills come with time, patience and experience. Developing an understanding of your prey and how to stalk it, along with building and using hides, can give you a much-needed edge over your quarry. The ability to utilize your senses to their full capacity will never be so important as when you are tracking. Hearing, smell, sight, touch, even taste – all will help to build up a picture of the animal's movements and actions, even its thought processes, as you use logic and instinct to track and follow your prey.

Sign

Sign – a recent indication of the presence of an animal or bird – is

Accuracy International Varmint

The British Accuracy International Company has long been known for its military sniper rifles. It also produces a range of target and hunting rifles using the same precision engineering. The Varmint is a high-grade hunting rifle made with a view to superb levels of accuracy within the limits of the selected calibres. Available calibres for the Varmint are .223 up to .308, and the gun is fitted with a 66cm (26in) stainless-steel fluted match-grade barrel (the barrel flutes reduce the weight of what is usually the heaviest part of any rifle). Being based upon a military weapon, the Varmint has a higher magazine capacity than many other bolt-action weapons – it can carry eight rounds. The ammunition box is detachable, and the cartridges inside it are staggered to reduce the depth of the box.

Everything about the Varmint is designed towards the ultimate precision shot. The trigger, for example, is match grade and has a two-stage design. Trigger pull weight itself ranges from 1.1 to 1.6kg (2.5 to 3.5lb), the weight being adjustable by the shooter. The bolt action is made to the highest tolerances, and development tests during production show that the action could fire 20,000

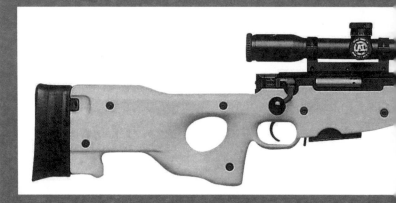

rounds without any serious malfunction. Nevertheless, Accuracy International makes all its parts interchangeable, and barrels can be swapped in a matter of minutes if necessary. Most other parts of the gun can be changed as well. The stock system is adjustable to fit the shooter, with spacers on the butt plate allowing the length of pull to be changed. (Stocks are available in various colours, from grey through to olive drab.)

The Varmint is not fitted with iron sights as standard (although they can be an option), but with a precision scope, it is a rifle with excellent hunting and target performance.

Specifications: Accuracy International Varmint
Calibre: .223–.308
Barrel length: 66cm (26in)
Weight: up to 6kg (13.2lb)
Sights: provision for scope
Mechanism: bolt action, magazine fed

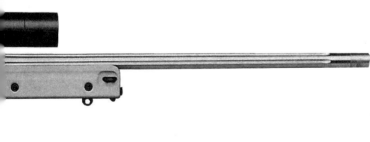

Hunting Kit

A well-equipped hunter should be prepared for whatever the outdoors decides to throw at him. Food, water, medical supplies and basic emergency camping kit should be packed for every trip.

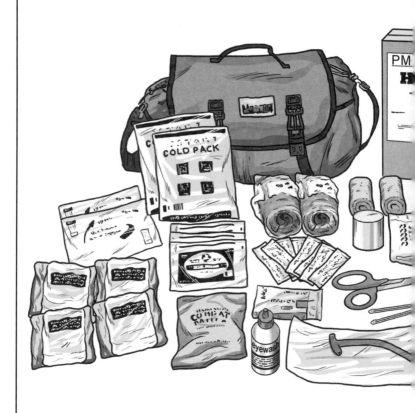

Be Properly Equipped

Before setting out on any shooting trip, you should ensure that you have suitable clothing, food and plenty of water, and at least a basic medical kit. This is most likely to be needed to deal with thorns and scrapes, but it is worth being able to clean and cover a cut whenever you are more than a few minutes from home. You should also find out about local wildlife hazards and the weather forecast, and take suitable precautions against getting lost. This might be nothing more than getting yourself a map, sticking it in a pocket and forgetting about it, but it will be there if you need it.

the element that dictates tracking. Sign effectively forms the markers by which you piece together the movement of an animal, and then use that information to track it to source or wait along one of its trails. The typical sorts of animal sign you can encounter are the following:

Disturbed Vegetation

Look for any signs that vegetation has been broken, displaced or otherwise modified by a passing animal. Branches might be snapped as an elk pushes through them; a bear can leave claw marks on trees to mark its territory, or might dig up roots and tubers; deer will strip the bark off tree saplings; or you might come across the husks of nuts left behind by squirrels. The height of broken vegetation will also give you a hint as to the size, and therefore species, of the animal. Essentially, look for anything that requires external force to perform, and use this along with other forms of sign to deduce which type of animal you are dealing with. (Swat up on the classic behaviours of your prey, so you can match sign to prey type.)

Droppings

Animal faeces can be one of the most direct signs that an animal is in an area. The internet will provide illustrative examples of the droppings of most types of animal, but there are some general principles you can follow to help with identification:

- Carnivorous and omnivorous animals usually produce long, tapering stools.
- Herbivores produce rounded dung piles matted with chewed vegetation.
- Birds that eat seeds, fruit and vegetation tend to make liquid dung.

- Carnivorous birds eating larger prey produce dry pellets.

Discarded Feathers, Fur or Bones

Feathers and fur can be caught on vegetation as an animal passes by, and both provide you with an excellent means of identifying the animals in an area. The same can also be found at kill sites, of course, which can help you identify both local predators and prey. Some creatures act as 'indicator' animals, whose presence indicates that a particular place is suitable for a wide variety of animal life. When voles and rabbits are prolific, for example, carnivorous animals are usually present too, and deer suggest that the vegetation food sources are plentiful and accessible.

Animal Tracks

Tracks are naturally the hunting sign par excellence. After all, you might successfully follow sign to find an animal, only to discover that it is not the animal you wished to hunt – recognizing animal tracks can prevent this from happening.

There are three main classifications of animals according to their feet: plantigrades, digitigrades and ungulates. Plantigrades include any animal that walks on the sole of its feet. These include humans and, in hunting terms, animals such as bears, rabbits, hares and badgers.

Evaluating Sign

A pile of animal droppings with clear tracks receding into the distance offer clear signs of animal movement.

Animal Gait

An animal's gait is dictated by its bone structure, and the tracks it leaves are dictated by its foot structure. Knowing at least a little about tracking can help avoid fruitless and frustrating trips where nothing was seen.

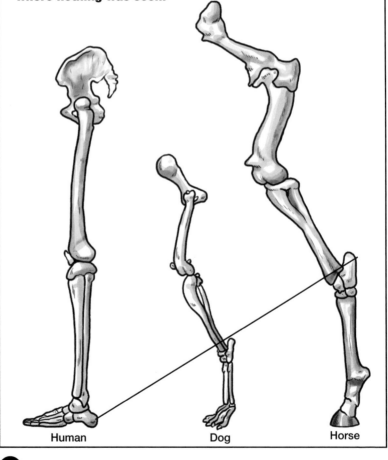

Human   Dog   Horse

Digitigrades walk on their toes and include any feline or canine. Ungulates are animals with hooves, where the toes have grown together to form either a solid or a cloven hoof. This group includes deer, sheep, goat, horses and cows.

Even if you can't spot an identifiable track, there can be some subtle signs that a creature has passed by. An animal crossing dewy grass knocks away moisture with each impact of the foot, creating a dull area. Leaves are compressed when walked upon and grit is pushed down into the surface of a track by the impact of a hoof. Try getting down to near floor level and scanning a trail with the light shining onto it from the other side – footmarks will often appear as either dull or shiny patches, depending on the contrast with the floor.

Vocalizations

The sounds of animals are very obvious indicators of their presence, from the grunts of a wild pig to the calls of a wild turkey hen. The volume and direction of the call can give you a lead as to the bearing of the hunt, although take care in mountainous or heavily wooded terrain, when the dynamics of sound in such echoing environments can fool your sense of direction.

Staying Hidden

Camouflage can greatly increase your chances of successfully stalking and tracking prey. There is a plethora of excellent camouflage clothing and equipment available for the hunter on today's market, including photo-realistic fabrics that authentically represent your backdrop. For good general lessons in camouflage, however, we can turn to military expertise. For soldiers, camouflage can mean the difference between safety, capture and even death. The following mnemonic covers the basics taught to most units:

'Seven S's'

- Shape
- Shine
- Silhouette
- Shadow
- Sound
- Speed
- Surroundings

These principles can be adapted specifically for tracking and hunting. Fundamentally, they involve breaking up the human silhouette and shape so that it is less recognizable and more in keeping with the natural surroundings. While human enemies will actively look for the shape of a helmet or boot prints, even animals can recognize a human shape or unnatural colours and textures, and may instinctively run from them. Therefore, altering your shape, colour and texture so that you blend in means that you are far less likely to stand out or attract attention, leaving you free to track your prey.

Browning BAR

The Browning BAR rifles hold the dominant position in the auto-loading rifle market, a position obtained through the quality of construction and the popularity of the available calibres. There are four basic models in the BAR range: the Long Trac and Short Trac (representing long-action and short-action rifles respectively), the Safari model and the new Stalker model. Differences between the models are mainly to do with construction and finish. The Safari model has a scroll-engraved ordnance steel receiver, while the other three models have plain aluminium alloy receivers.

The composite stocks of stalker guns are also rendered in a matte black finish, whereas the Short Trac and Long Trac come in either natural wood or Mossy Oak New Break-Up camouflage. Across the guns the available calibres include .243 Win, .25-06, .30-06 Springfield, .270 Win, .270 WSM, 7mm WSM, 7mm Mag, 7mm Rem Mag, .300 Win Mag, .308 and .338 Win Mag. This selection of calibres covers almost all the bases for hunters who want to take on everything from deer through to moose and safari game.

BAR rifles are gas-operated auto-loaders. The bolt locks into the barrel via seven lugs on its head and the bolt face is also recessed to grip the end of the cartridge very firmly, thus ensuring controlled

feeding and a stable seating in the chamber. BAR rifles are known for their accuracy, and this can be further improved through the option of the Ballistic Optimizing Shooting System (BOSS). This is essentially an adjustable muzzle brake/weight system that can be configured to tune out vibrations, which can impair accuracy, hence improving the stability of the bullet flight. (Browning also make the BOSS CR system, which has the weight-adjusting features but without the muzzle brake.) Recoil control in the BAR guns is also excellent.

All of the BAR rifles have receivers that are drilled and tapped for scope mounts, but the Lightweight Stalker model comes with open sights as standard. These consist of a rear click-adjustable sight corresponding with a hooded front bead.

Specifications: Browning BAR Long Trac
Calibre: .270 Win, .30-06 Springfield, 7mm Rem. Mag, .300 Win Mag
Barrel length: 56cm (22in), 61cm (24in)
Weight: up to 3.4kg (7.5lb)
Sights: receiver drilled and tapped for scope
Mechanism: gas operated

Comprehensive Camouflage

Good camouflage
softens or alters the
distinctive outline of
the human form, but
it must be extended
to the rifle as well or
much of the benefit
is lost. A few scraps
of cloth or some
vegetation would
make this weapon
a lot less obvious.

The easiest way to camouflage yourself is with professionally made clothing. Yet the hunting process can take you through areas of contrasting terrain, when the ability to improvise becomes important. Such is our focus here.

Shape, Colour and Texture

Visual camouflage essentially strives to break up the human shape so that it disperses more naturally into its surroundings. You can easily do this by adding pieces of vegetation or strips of natural coloured fabric to your clothing, headgear and equipment, so that your relatively smooth outline is broken up (nature contains very few smooth lines). The more your shape crumples into the background, the less noticeable it is.

For particularly vigilant prey, such as wild turkey, you may also need to camouflage your gun. As mentioned, there are few straight lines in nature, so a gleaming, ramrod-straight gun barrel will be conspicuous. You can buy guns that are already camouflaged, but you can also improvise by wrapping camouflage fabric or netting around key points of the weapon. Whatever modifications you make, however, make sure you don't obscure the operating mechanism or the sights.

Shine, Shadow and Silhouette

Do not forget to dull any exposed skin such as your face and hands,

Camouflaging Your Weapon

The stock of a weapon will be concealed against the user's body, but the fore end sticks out quite a long way. Camouflage should blur the outlines of the gun but must not impede the action or cover the sights.

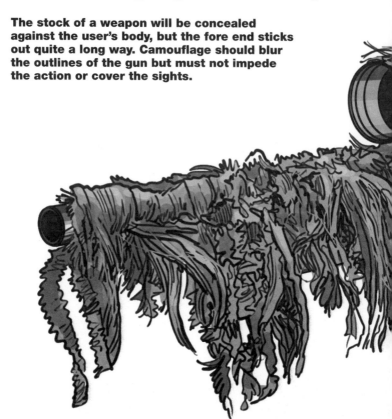

which can stand out remarkably clearly, especially when bathed with sweat. Charcoal made by burning paper or wood is useful if you do not have shop-bought camouflage paint.

Apply the camouflage in an irregular pattern that suits your environment. The best skin camouflage uses a variety of shades to mirror the contrasting backdrop found in nature,

with more prominent features, such as forehead, nose, chin and ears, coloured more darkly. Shaded areas, such as under the eyes or chin, can be coloured in a lighter hue.

Shadow can be a great help when tracking, as it conceals colour, silhouette and shine. The deeper the shadow, the darker it is, so use it to your advantage – along with

Face Camouflage

Face camouflage can disguise the outlines and distinctive features of the head, and also alters the colour of flesh. This can be important when hunting animals that can be spooked by bare skin.

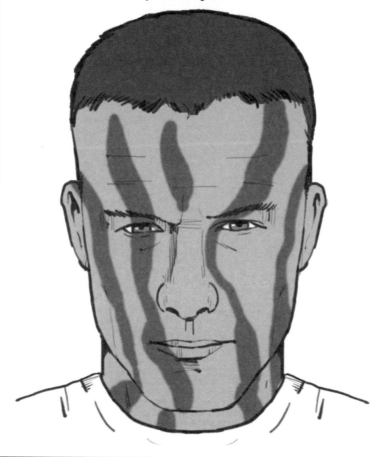

vegetation where possible – for concealment. Shadows can also form useful passing points when you are moving across gaps in terrain, as walking through them will make it harder for you to be spotted.

Sound

Inevitably, most movements will cause some level of sound, and birds and animals will flee from sudden, loud or unfamiliar noises. At the very least they will cause prey to exercise much more caution and to be more vigilant.

You can minimize the chances of being heard even before you begin tracking. When dressed in your camouflage, carrying your equipment, jump up and down on the spot a few times. You will be able to instantly identify any audible clues that could give your position away while you are on the move. If you find something that jangles, taps or otherwise makes a noise, remove it or tie/tape it down. Ensure that any electronic devices that might emit a noise are turned on to silent beforehand. The sound of a phone or watch alarm going off, plus your attempts to muffle it, will instantly send your quarry running for safety.

Stalking

Stalking you prey once it is spotted requires patience and nerve. Your objective is to put yourself within a workable range for your primary weapon, which might be a few dozen metres or perhaps hundreds of metres. In essence, you have to think of yourself as an animal, soundlessly but ruthlessly pursuing its prey, but also using every ounce of your intelligence to outwit the superior

It's Not Just About the Guns

It is surprisingly common for shooters to forget about basics like sun, wind and rain, despite having every conceivable hunting accessory and a selection of the finest guns available. Common-sense precautions against needless disasters are really nothing to do with shooting; they are what everyone should do when heading out into the countryside. A shooting trip is no different to camping or hiking in that regard – don't let the guns distract you from other basic concerns.

Stalking

Staying low, moving slowly and remaining downwind of the animal will assist in reaching a shooting position. However careful you are, stalking is a painstaking process that often has to be repeated because some random factor caused the quarry to move away.

senses the animal will undoubtedly possess.

The route you choose is of paramount importance to the success of a hunt. Choose and follow a route that gives you maximum cover, utilizing features such as ditches, large trees, sections of bush, deep foliage, rocky outcrops or the reverse side of hills.

Be on the lookout for gaps in cover that could cause you to expose yourself briefly. In the same way, any obstacles must be factored in – don't attempt to stalk a creature across large or difficult obstacles, as you are almost certain to make noise during the effort of crossing them.

Just keep as close to the natural shape of the terrain as possible. Alternative routes should also be planned out in your mind's eye for when your quarry or the wind changes direction, or if your way becomes blocked.

One key point about the stalking process is to stay downwind of the animal you are hunting, so that wind strikes the animal before it hits you. If you position yourself upwind, your scent will be carried to alert nostrils and the animal will disappear quickly.

Putting yourself downwind of the animal might involve a considerable detour, but there are few shortcuts to stalking if you want to put yourself in an advantageous position for a kill.

Small Game

Small game such as rabbit and squirrel might not appear as the most satisfying of kills, but what they lack in individual meat content, they more than make up for in proliferation. For hunting with a gun, the process is more a case of moving carefully and slowly through the wilderness, keeping a watchful eye out for movement and being ready to take the shot at any moment. The ideal gun for such small game is a .22 air rifle, a .22 rimfire rifle or a 20- or 12-gauge shotgun loaded with No.5 to 7½ shot, depending on the size of the prey you intend to hunt.

When hunting for rabbits and hares, check through undergrowth, woodpiles, bushes, thick grass and anywhere else the animals are likely to hide. You might suddenly flush the creature from cover; take the shot quickly, as once the animal builds its run up to full speed, it can be surprisingly hard to hit.

Deer Hunting

Deer are one of the world's most popular animals to hunt, and also one of the most demanding. Most species of deer are highly sensitive creatures, jumpy and alert to even the slightest changes in their environment or to minor movements in the terrain. For this reason, the successful hunting of deer requires excellent fieldcraft skills, the right equipment and a deep knowledge of their species-specific

Head Shot

For small game at close ranges, a head shot can be one of the best options for quick dispatch, and means that no meat is lost.

White-tailed Deer

Although white-tailed deer can be successfully hunted with muzzle-loaders or even bows, most hunters use a fairly powerful rifle to ensure a clean kill without having to get so close that the deer may be spooked. Many hunters recommend .30-06 or .308 as ideal for deer.

behaviour. Make sure that you have a rifle capable of handling the deer you intend to hunt. The calibre can vary tremendously, as deer range in adult body weight from 10kg (22lb) to several hundred kilograms, depending on the species. The right calibre to use will often be dictated by local or national hunting legislation, but check first with a reputable gun store or experienced hunter.

For a clean kill, you want to put your shot into the animal's heart, lungs or spine (its central nervous system). If the animal is presented from the side, the main target areas are just above the foreleg or along the ridge of the neck. The former will bring the deer down quite quickly as the bullet hits the heart and lungs, whereas the latter will drop it instantly on the spot. If shooting the animal from the front, an impact point between the forelegs ensures direct impact on the internal organs, and shooting from behind presents the back of the neck as the best target. Fix your sights on the impact point, breathe steadily and squeeze out the shot.

In an ideal world the shot will take out the deer instantly. The animal might fall over, then run a few metres and take cover behind a tree or bush. In these situations, don't spring up immediately and start running after the creature – this will just encourage it to use its dying energy to get away from you, making it harder for you to track. After about three minutes, get

Marlin Model 980S

The .22 Long Rifle (LR) round is popular among new and experienced shooters alike, and the Marlin Model 980S is an excellent rimfire gun for basic pest control and hunting. Marlin produces an especially broad range of small-gauge rifles, and the quality of these firearms means the company commands strong sectors of the market. Its guns include automatic-loading .17 and .22 rifles such as the Model 60, Model 7000 and Model 717M2, a classic lever-action .22, the Golden 39A and the rifle featured here, the Model 980S. This is a bolt-action rifle chambered only for .22LR, the gun being fed from a seven-shot nickel-plated clip magazine. A thumb-operated switch provides safety, and the gun also has a red cocking indicator.

Marlin rimfire rifles all feature the T-900 Fire Control System, which Marlin promotes as an exceptional new trigger-system improvement over existing models. It has a wide, serrated trigger for positive trigger contact, a crisp single-stage trigger pull and a safety that acts upon the trigger itself.

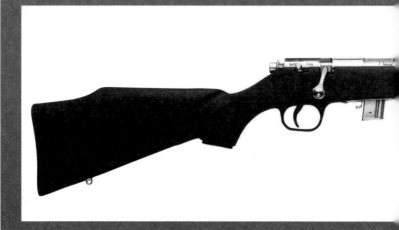

The barrel features Micro-Groove rifling that gives the gun great accuracy over the 100m (328ft) practical range of the rimfire round. Sights on the barrel are an adjustable semi-buckhorn folding rear sight corresponding with a ramped front sight (with an orange front sight post) and cutaway Wide-Scan hood. The 980S overall is a compact gun, measuring 104cm (41in). Its weight is also kept to a manageable level – approximately 2.7kg (6lb). Nickel-plated swivel studs are also provided.

Specifications: Marlin Model 980S
Calibre: .22LR
Barrel length: 56cm (22in)
Weight: 2.7kg (6lb)
Sights: fixed front and rear; drilled and tapped for scope mount
Mechanism: bolt action, magazine fed

Mountain Goat

A good choice for hunting goats is a rifle chambered in .243 or a similar calibre. Goats can be encountered at various distances and in varied terrain, so an all-round gun is useful.

up and walk towards the spot where you saw the deer hit. Hopefully it will be lying dead not far from this point (or on the spot itself); touch its eye with a stick or knife to see if there is a reaction, indicating that it is not quite dead.

Any wounded animal should be dispatched immediately, either by a shot to the back of the neck (at such close ranges, sight along the side of the barrel rather than use the telescopic sight) or, if you have the experience and the animal is not thrashing about dangerously, by cutting its throat.

Wild Sheep and Goats

You are rarely likely to take a close-range shot against a wild sheep or goat, hence you need a rifle that can deliver a good long-range punch at a flat trajectory. As there is some considerable variation in the size and weight of wild sheep and goats, you will also need to take expert advice before purchase of weapon and ammunition. Typically, goats require

U.S. Army Tip – Upright Stalking

Take steps about half your normal stride when stalking in an upright position. Such strides help you to maintain your balance. You should be able to stop at any point in that movement and hold that position as long as necessary. Curl the toes up out of the way when stepping down, so the outside edge of the ball of the foot touches the ground. Feel for sticks and twigs that may snap when you place your weight on them. If you start to step on one, lift your foot and move it. After making contact with the outside edge of the ball of your foot, roll to the inside ball of your foot, place your heel down, followed by your toes. Then gradually shift your weight forward to the front foot. Lift the back foot to about knee height and start the process over again. Keep your hands and arms close to your body and avoid waving them about or hitting vegetation. When moving in a crouch, you gain extra support by placing your hands on your knees. One step usually takes one minute to complete, but the time it takes will depend on the situation.

– U.S. Army, FM 3-05.70, Survival (2002)

heavier calibres than sheep, such as the 7mm/.270, .30-06 or .308.

Stalking is generally the only method of hunting these creatures. Given the nature of the terrain, you should only attempt to hunt in mountains if you have experience or if you are in the company of a seasoned guide. Put safety first at all times, and don't attempt to negotiate terrain that presents a significant danger from rockfalls, avalanches or drops.

For stalking wild sheep and goat, the best method is to find a good vantage spot on the upper slopes, hidden from view where possible, and scan the lower slopes with a pair of powerful binoculars or spotting scope. A keen eye is essential here, as wild sheep and goats often blend effortlessly into the background. If one is spotted just out of shot range, you need to close the distance by moving up to a shooting point with extreme stealth, staying out of view as much as you can. When you do get into a position to take the shot, make sure that if the animal falls, it won't tumble away out of reach – there is no point in shooting an animal if you cannot safely retrieve it afterwards.

Wild Boar

Wild boar is an exciting prospect for the hunter. They can be genuinely dangerous animals, being heavy (some species can reach weights of more than 300kg/661lb), aggressive and armed with extremely sharp

Wild Boar

Boars are tough and can be extremely dangerous. A powerful rifle of at least .270 calibre is recommended, or a 12-gauge shotgun.

tusks that can inflict serious flesh wounds on an opponent. Although attacks on humans by wild boar are relatively rare, when threatened or wounded they can make a potentially lethal charge.

Boar tend to live in forest regions, and are elusive animals. Signs of their presence include tracks (particularly around watering holes), disturbed earth (they like to dig for roots and tubers), faeces and mud wallows. In terms of hunting methods, the hunter can stalk on his own or in a small group (which is recommended), although given the sensitivity of the animal to noise and movement, this process needs performing with a very steady and careful approach.

Whatever the hunting method, the choice of weapon is important for wild boar. Cartridges such as the .270, .30-06 and .308 are all practical, depending on the boar species, and shotgun slugs are also effective at close ranges. The shot is usually taken over open sights for fast target acquisition, and some hunters prefer to use a semi-auto weapon, providing a rapid follow-up shot if the boar makes a charge. An alternative, popular in Europe, is a three-barrelled weapon known as a combination gun, which combines a rifle barrel and two shotgun barrels – the rifle provides a longer-range reach while the shotgun components enable the hunter to take on the boar at close ranges.

Northern Caribou

Caribou (or reindeer) require a powerful rifle. Weapons in the .30-06 range are effective, and some hunters recommend .444 Marlin as an ideal choice for caribou hunting. This is essentially an upscacled .44 Magnum handgun round, with a longer cartridge and more propellant for greater hitting power.

Mannlicher Pro Hunter

The Pro Hunter is a serious range of rifles for tough outdoor use. All parts of the weapons are designed for both high accuracy in the final shot and for durability against environmental conditions. They are fitted out with a synthetic black or grey stock that is impervious to wet and cold (the stock can be reinforced with fibreglass as an option at additional cost). Stock stability is extremely important in a hunting rifle, because any warping in the stock material can affect the true straightness of the barrel or the seating of the action.

The length of pull (LOP) of the stock can also be adjusted simply by adding or removing the provided stock spacers – these take the LOP from around 32cm (12.8in) out to 35cm (13.8in). The magazine is made of a synthetic material, and a high-capacity 10-round adaptor is available for this. Regarding the word 'undestroyable', Steyr Mannlicher use it to refer to the 'matte metal surface finish

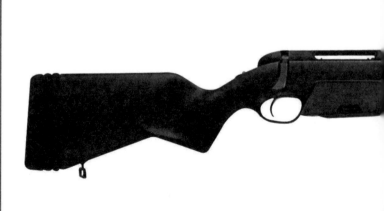

[that] guarantees perfect anti-corrosion protection, as well as enhanced durability against mechanical strain'.

Calibre options are typically wide, from .222 Rem up to .300 Win Mag. The barrel length of the standard calibre is 60cm (23.6in), while for the magnum calibres another 5cm (2in) of barrel length is added.

Specifications: Mannlicher Pro Hunter
Calibre: 14 calibres from .222 Rem to .300 Win Mag
Barrel length: 60cm (23.6in), 65cm (25.6in)
Weight: up to 3.7kg (8.2lb)
Sights: provision for scope
Mechanism: bolt action, magazine fed

Moose

Moose require a large-calibre rifle to take down cleanly. May hunters recommend .30-06 or .308 rifles, or others in the same class. Smaller rifles are unlikely to do more than wound the animal.

Large American/ Eurasian Ungulates

Ungulates such as caribou, elk and moose are substantial kills for any hunter and make an excellent food source for a group of people. They are often some of the best meat available in an otherwise stark wilderness environment. The American elk is a sizeable deer. Its sub-species show some size variation, but the largest variety – the Roosevelt elk – can weigh up to 600kg (1320lb) and stand more than 1.5m (5ft) at the shoulder. Given their size and power, elk need a powerful gun to bring them down with confidence, something in the region of .30-06 or .300 Magnum.

Bear

Bear hunting, as with many forms of large game hunting, is heavily restricted in many countries. Rightly so, for unrestricted hunting led to the decimation of global bear populations, and even today many species are threatened by illegal hunting, especially in Eastern Europe and Asia. When bear hunting is allowed it must be done respectfully, both because of the magnificence of the animal and because of the dangers involved. A wounded bear at close range is a terrifying prospect, and one that could easily kill a complacent hunter. In terms of the rifles used to bring down bear, practical calibres include .270, .308, .30-06 and .358 Winchester, which are all fit for purpose.

Grizzly Bear

Bears are extremely dangerous, with thick hide and muscle that can stop a less powerful round. Large-calibre rifles chambered for .375 or .450 are recommended by many hunters, with shotguns or large calibre handguns as an emergency backup if a wounded bear attacks the hunters.

Bears in remote wilderness settings can be extremely wily and difficult to spot. They also have a sharp sense of smell and hearing, although their eyesight isn't particularly acute. Your first step in hunting bear, therefore, is to identify an area in which

they are found. Often you can do this with the advice of local guides, but physical signs include the following:

- Tracks and scat
- Signs of digging for roots and tubers

Hunting in West Virginia. One consideration when choosing a rifle for hunting is that you will have to carry it.

- Carcasses of animals exhibiting major claw and teeth marks
- Claw or teeth marks on trees, created by bears marking their territory
- Trails leading naturally through woodland or forest

If you do come across such signs, especially if they are fresh, have your rifle at the ready, as bears could be close by and might not take kindly to your wandering through their territory. Otherwise, try to find vantage spots from which you can scan the terrain with binoculars or your scope, trying to spot a bear. Be especially vigilant if you spot an animal carcass. Watch this point for some time, because bears are natural scavengers and might reveal themselves when they come out to feed.

When the opportunity for a shot arises, only take it if you are extremely confident of a solid, deep-penetrating hit in a vital area. If you have a bolt-action rifle, reload straight away and prepare for a follow-up shot. Needless to say, approach an apparently dead bear with extreme caution, monitoring for any signs of movement and keeping your weapon at the ready.

Modern firearms use nitrocellulose-based propellants that are quite difficult to ignite. At the time of their invention, late in the nineteenth century, these new 'smokeless propellants' were something of a revolution, especially in military applications. It became possible to fire repeated shots without vast clouds of billowing smoke obscuring the entire battlefield. For military and 'serious' applications such as hunting for the table, modern propellants rapidly displaced traditional black powder. However, there remains a significant section of the shooting community who enjoy the challenge of black-powder shooting or relish the experience of shooting historical guns.

Black Powder Weaponry

Black powder is much easier to ignite than modern propellants – a spark will do it most of the time (though it seems that powder has the ability to become inert whenever it really matters that a shot goes off). It also burns much more slowly than nitrocellulose, which alters the firing characteristics of the weapon.

Black powder is still manufactured, though there are modern versions that are a little safer to store and which can be formed into convenient

. . . .

A hunter shoots at fowl using a percussion cap rifle in this nineteenth century illustration.

8

Most gun sports are undertaken with efficient modern weapons, but many shooters enjoy recreational shooting with more primitive weapons. Often, it is the experience rather than the outcome that is important.

Black Powder and Antique Weapons

M1841 Mississippi Rifle

The M1841 Mississippi rifle was the first US service rifle to adopt percussion-cap technology. It remains popular as a historically-significant weapon for recreational shooting and hunting.

pellets. These substitutes can be used in most black powder weapons, unlike modern propellants, which are not safe for use in weapons not designed for their use. Black powder is formed into grains, with finer grains burning faster than coarse powder. Faster-burning powder is primarily used in short-barrel weapons and some small-calibre rifles, with slower powder being suitable for larger bore rifles, shotguns and muskets.

Flintlocks

Various designs of black powder weapons have been produced over the centuries, but most black powder shooting today uses either flintlock or percussion ignition. A flintlock uses a piece of flint to strike sparks off an upright piece of steel called the frizzen. The resulting shower of sparks falls into a small amount of fine gunpowder that is held in the 'pan', hopefully igniting it. Since, however, the powder in the pan is

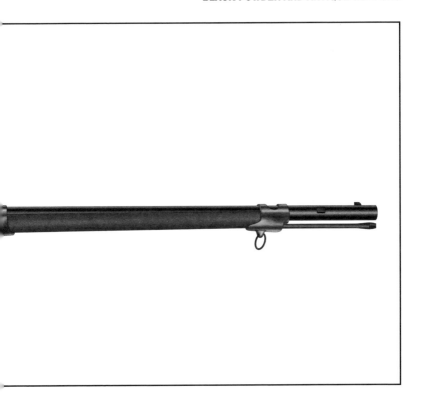

exposed to wind and damp, there are no guarantees that this will happen, even if the flint is in good shape.

If the powder in the priming pan does ignite, then hopefully flame passes through a small hole (the touch-hole) to ignite the main charge and send the projectile on its way. Sometimes all that happens is that the priming powder burns – this is where the phrase 'a flash in the pan' comes from – and the main charge is not ignited. It

may be possible to prime the pan again and have another go, but just because the weapon does not immediately fire does not mean that it is not going to – hang-fires are quite common with black powder weapons, and it is entirely possible that the powder may ignite later, a few seconds after the trigger is pulled. Learning to deal with misfires and hang-fires is an essential part of black powder shooting.

Flintlock Mechanism

A flintlock weapon relies on striking a flint against the frizzen to create a shower of sparks that will (hopefully) ignite the powder in the pan. A badly shaped flint, damp powder or a host of other things can cause the weapon to misfire.

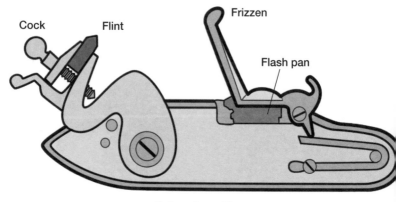

Full cock position

Percussion Caps

The other common black powder weapon type uses percussion ignition. In this case the mechanism is quite similar, but instead of a lock holding a piece of flint, the firing mechanism is a hammer which falls onto a percussion cap located roughly where the frizzen would be on a flintlock. The cap is initiated by a sharp blow of the hammer, sending flame into the main charge and, hopefully, igniting it.

Percussion-cap weapons are vastly more reliable than flintlocks, but that is still relative. Compared to a modern firearm, percussion-locks are highly prone to misfires and inexplicable malfunctions, though they are much less susceptible to damp than flintlocks. Both are muzzle-loaders, in which the main charge is poured down the barrel and followed by the projectile(s), which are held in place with a wad. This part of the loading process is

Ignition

Cock released position

much the same for both flintlocks and percussion weapons.

Percussion (or cap-and-ball) revolvers are not muzzle-loaders but instead require a fairly lengthy process of loading each chamber in turn. This is done with the hammer at half-cock, allowing the cylinder to turn. Powder is poured into the chamber and followed with a ball, and the chambers are then sealed with grease. This prevents chain-fires, in which the ignition of one chamber sets off the others. Since these other chambers are not lined up with the barrel, the results are always destructive.

Finally, the firing nipples are fitted with a cap, readying the weapon for use. Since cap-and-ball revolvers traditionally had no safety system, the chamber under the hammer was often left empty. Cocking the hammer rotates a loaded chamber into position, so the weapon can be carried in this condition but still be ready to fire. Some designs are safe to carry with six loaded and capped chambers.

Percussion Cap Mechanism

Percussion rifles are muzzle-loaded with black powder, but use a percussion cap to ignite it. This makes them somewhat more reliable than flintlocks. The hammer mechanism was originally adapted from the flintlock.

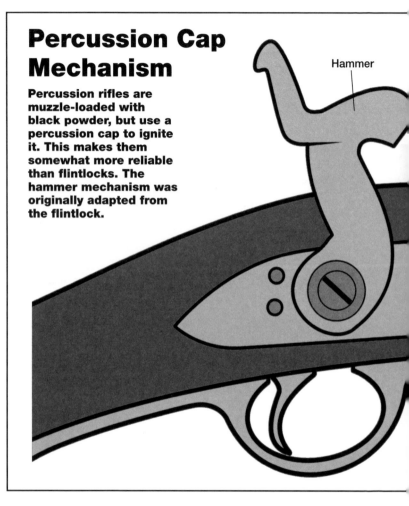

Hammer

Loading

It is always wise to use a powder measure when loading any black powder weapon. With revolvers it is generally possible to judge the load by eye, but this is much more difficult with long guns. It is possible to overload a black powder weapon to a dangerous degree, and in any case using a measure or

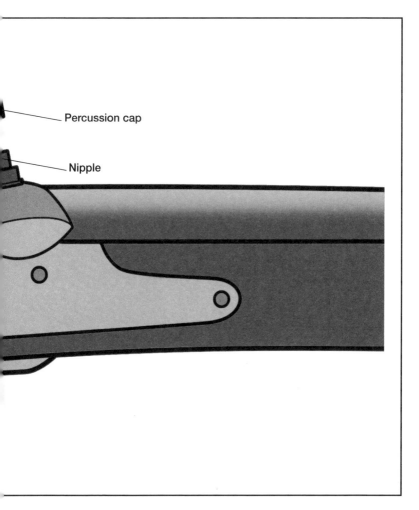

Percussion cap

Nipple

a pre-prepared charge means that only a single shot's worth of powder is taken close to the gun. This can prevent disaster if sparks remain present after a shot.

Black powder is horribly corrosive, so guns must be cleaned thoroughly after even a couple of shots. They also foul quickly, and may need attention if a large number of shots

Whitworth Rifle

The Whitworth rifle, although a muzzle-loading black powder design, was sufficiently accurate to be used as a sniping weapon with a range of over 1000m (1094yds).

Baker Rifle

The Baker Rifle was used by some British troops in the Napoleonic era, and more widely later. It is accurate to several hundred metres, though being a flintlock, it is not as reliable as some later weapons.

Smoothbore Balls and Minie Bullets

Musket balls are inaccurate – and not just because they rattle around in the bore as they proceed up the barrel. They lose energy quickly and can vary considerably in trajectory. The Minie bullet solved this problem by having a hollow base. Expanding propellant gases caused the bullet to widen at the base, gripping the weapon's rifling to impart spin.

are fired. Hot soapy water is fine for getting rid of powder residue, followed by treatment with a lubricant optimized for black powder weapons.

Shooting With Black Powder Weapons

Many black powder shooters engage in what would be fairly standard target shooting or 'plinking', were it not for the additional difficulty of using an unreliable and temperamental weapon. A black powder shooter once told me, 'Most shooters care about the size of their group. Some days, just getting the weapon to fire is enough for me!'

In addition to the aesthetic appeal of shooting a historical weapon, black powder shooting is a real challenge. Many shooters use flintlock muskets, which are smoothbore weapons firing a ball that is not a tight fit in the barrel and are therefore not the most precise instruments ever invented. This creates – or perhaps requires – different expectations compared to someone who routinely gets through hundreds of rounds in an afternoon. Loading takes time, but if it is seen as part of the black powder shooting experience, then that is not a problem. Impatience to get the weapon ready for a shot will lead to frustration, and probably a poorly aimed shot as well.

Thus, shooting a musket is a very deliberate exercise, and even

Renato Gamba Ambassador

It is arguable that if you can spend up to $10,000 on a shotgun, then any weapon priced beyond that will give you nothing extra in terms of functionality and performance. Nevertheless, the lure of shotgun excellence is strong, and there remain plenty of investors in the market for guns priced upwards of $100,000 – and even beyond. Although such purchases are rarely fired, many are bought as collector's pieces to hold and improve their value over many years. What you get is exquisite appearance, rock solid and often hand-finished engineering, and pure joy to shoot.

A review on the Internet of the Ambassador sidelock discovered the sale of one example, built in 1979 and formerly owned by Prince Faisal M. Al Saud, with a price tag of over $56,000, although other second-hand models are available closer to the region of $15,000. The Ambassador itself is a 66cm (26in) or 71cm (28in) side-by-side gun. It has demi-bloc barrels, meaning that the lumps are forged integrally with the barrel they join, the two barrel sets then being set together.

Demi-bloc barrels have a very favourable strength-to-weight ratio, and they also allow close setting of the barrels at the breech end, so that it is easier to regulate the point of aim for the pair of barrels. A three-bite double Purdey locking system is used, single or double triggers can be ordered, and the woodwork is of the finest quality. The gun is made with a personalized fit, and it is doubtless something the shooter will treasure for many years.

Specifications: Renato Gamba Ambassador
Gauge/calibre: 12
Barrel length: 66cm (26in), 71cm (28in)
Weight: depends on stock dimensions
Ejector type: automatic ejectors
Chokes: fixed
Features: demi-bloc construction

a well-aimed shot can go a fair way off target – assuming a hang-fire or misfire does not occur. The sort of shooter who becomes frustrated with his weapon is not going to enjoy the experience. Black powder target shooting is definitely for those who enjoy the whole experience rather than those who obsess about results.

That does not, however, preclude some fairly intense competition. The use of uniform ammunition and carefully measured powder charges removes some of the variance, and although a musket will never be a paragon of accuracy, if the playing field is level, then it is still possible to have an intense competition of skill.

Rifled Weapons

Accuracy is greatly enhanced by using a rifled weapon, whether a flintlock or a percussion type. Many hunters favour black powder rifles for hunting, not least for the additional challenge. The accurate range of a black powder rifle is not, on the whole, great, so when hunting it is best to take only short-range shots where a clean kill is likely. For weapons firing a ball, this means 100m (328ft) or less, with 150m (490ft) being the outer limit for conical bullets. A marginal hit may be possible, even likely, at greater distances but it is not humane to have wounded animals running off while you reload.

Shotguns

Black powder shotguns are also popular in some quarters. Black powder is less potent than modern propellants, so muzzle velocities are lower with all weapons. With a shotgun, that means it is necessary to shorten the range at which you shoot a given target, compared to a modern gun. Shot loses velocity fast and will spread out more over a given distance – and, of course, it will take longer to reach the aim point, giving the target more time to move.

All these factors make black powder shotgunning a real challenge, but nevertheless (or perhaps because of these factors) it remains a popular pastime. A black powder shotgun can be used to hunt or to shoot clay pigeons, and in skilled hands is about as effective as a modern shotgun within its limits.

Competitions

Specialist black powder shooting competitions exist, with divisions and subdivisions for various weapon types. In most cases any black powder suitable for its category can be used, whether it is an antique, a replica or a modern black powder weapon. The only definite require-ment is for the weapon to be safe to shoot. Sights must be contemporary for the weapon; there are no laser sights in black powder shooting, even if one would be useful in all that smoke.

Pistol, rifle and shotgun competi-tions are all held, with varying rules.

Some allow nitrocellulose propellants to be used where appropriate; many do not. Some target rifle events are held at ranges that would challenge many modern guns – 500–1000m (540–1080yds). In longer-range events, participants are often allowed to take as many ranging shots as they please before firing 'for record', providing they can complete their shoot within a set period.

Black powder weapons (mainly cap-and-ball or percussion types) are used in Cowboy Action Shooting events. Black powder is not greatly inferior to modern propellants for short-range, point-and-shoot events, and of course the smoke and the smell are all part of an authentic experience. Indeed, for many shooters black powder shooting is all about the experience – it's not about hitting the target, it's about enjoying all the things you have to do as you try to hit the target.

Bloodless Duelling

Until the late nineteenth century, pistols were used for duelling. Traditionally, these were perfectly matched flintlocks. A pistol duel was potentially lethal, but the weapons were sufficiently inaccurate that even a well-aimed shot might miss – and many duellists deliberately fired into the air. For those who did not feel that it was enough to satisfy honour by confronting death in this manner, and who actually tried to hit their opponent, it proved harder than expected. The fear that comes with facing a live pistol at short range made it very difficult to aim properly.

As pistols replaced swords as the weapon of choice for duelling,

'Fouling Shots'

Peculiarities of black powder shooting competitions include the use of 'fouling shots' at the beginning of an event. A weapon shoots differently with powder residue in the barrel to when it is completely clean, and a fouling shot ensures that the weapon's performance on the first shot is not wildly different to the next. Often, events count only a set number of the best shots from each weapon, with a larger number allowed. This eliminates some of the vagaries of black powder, whereby an otherwise well-aimed shot can be ruined by uneven burning of powder or other uncontrollable factors.

some fencing schools began offering training in the art of pistol duelling, and invented a means to practise safely. This became known as 'bloodless duelling' and used replica flintlock pistols powered by compressed air, firing wax bullets.

This allowed potential duellists to practise both their marksmanship and to develop a steady nerve in the face of a weapon, without much danger of injury. Bloodless duelling was not painless duelling, of course. Being hit with a high-speed ball of wax was very painful, despite protective equipment consisting of a long coat, a fencing mask and goggles. Not surprisingly, it was turned into a sport.

The last bloodless duelling competition was held around 1908, but recently the sport has been revived. In October 2012, I took part in the first competition of the revival, going out in the second round to a 'mutual death'. As gun sports go, shooting at other human beings is a bit extreme, but it may be that in time, bloodless duelling will become a more widespread activity.

As with other shooting sports, bloodless duelling uses the traditional techniques and the weapons are replicas in form, if not in exact func-tion, of the standard duelling pistol. This perhaps contradicts the rule that a 'sporting gun' is one designed for other purposes than shooting at human beings, but there are always exceptions to any rule.

Bloodless Duelling

Protected by a long coat, mask and a handguard, duellists can practise their skills for the real thing, or recreational shooters can find out what it is like to take aim at a human being while being shot back at. The experience is... interesting.

Glossary

Action – The working mechanism of a firearm, responsible for the main activities of loading, firing and ejecting.

Blowback operated – A system used in automatic weapons, where the pressure on the cartridge case provides the energy to operate the loading and unloading cycle of the weapon when the gun is fired.

Bolt – The part of a rifle or semi-auto shotgun that pushes the cartridge into the chamber and locks it in place, and through which runs the firing pin.

Bore – The interior section of a gun's barrel.

Boxlock – A type of action in a break-open gun where all of the lockwork is contained within a box-like housing. Boxlocks are the most common type of double-barrelled shotgun mechanism, being relatively inexpensive to manufacture and extremely robust.

Breech – The rear part of a barrel into which a cartridge is inserted.

Centrefire – A cartridge that has the percussion cap located directly in the centre of the cartridge base.

Choke – The constriction, of various diameters, at the muzzle end of a smooth bore weapon that helps control the spread of the shot through the air. Chokes can be fixed (the muzzle is built to the desired choke specification) or interchangeable (the choke can be altered by means of screw-in muzzle inserts).

Comb – The top of a gunstock, where the shooter's cheek sits when the gun is mounted.

Ejector – A system for throwing the spent cartridge cases from a gun.

Extractor – A system for lifting spent cartridge cases out of the chambers, making them easily removed by hand.

Fluted barrel – A barrel with longitudinal depressions cut into its surface, which reduce the overall weight of the barrel and improve cooling.

Fore-end – The front part of a stock, usually located under the barrel.

Free-floating – A barrel is free-floating if it is not in contact with the fore-end; this reduces barrel distortion and improves accuracy.

Furniture – External metal fittings on a gun, such as trigger guard, sling swivels, etc.

Gas operated – An automatic weapon that uses burnt propellant gases to operate the cycle of loading and unloading.

Gauge – The calibre of a shotgun bore. The term relates to the number of lead balls the same diameter as the bore that it takes to make 1lb (0.45kg) in weight.

Hammer – In a long gun, the part of a gun that strikes the firing pin, driving it onto the percussion cap.

Lock – The system of securing a cartridge in the chamber to ensure that it is safe to fire.

Monobloc – The solid block at the end of some shotgun barrels into which the breech ends are machined.

Over-and-under – In a double-barrel shotgun, where the barrels are set one on top of the other in a vertical plane.

Receiver – The basic structure of a gun that houses the working parts and on to which the barrel and stock are assembled. Sometimes also called the 'action'.

Recoil operated – A gun that uses the forces of recoil to operate the loading and unloading cycle.

Rib – A metal platform running along shotgun barrels that acts as a sighting plane.

Rimfire – Cartridges that have the primer distributed around the rim of the cartridge head.

Sear – A part of the trigger mechanism that holds back the hammer, striker or firing pin in the cocked position until released.

Set trigger – A trigger that can be 'set' so that a light touch fires the gun.

Side-by-side – In a double-barrel shotgun, where the barrels are set side-by-side on a horizontal plane.

Sidelock – A shotgun mechanism that has the action mounted on removable sideplates.

INDEX

Page numbers in *italics* refer to illustrations.

Picture Credits